BRIAN JOHNSTON

Sowing in Hard Soil

Tools and Encouragement for Preaching the Gospel

First published by Hayes Press 2020

Copyright © 2020 by Brian Johnston

All rights reserved. No part of this publication may be reproduced, stored or transmitted in any form or by any means, electronic, mechanical, photocopying, recording, scanning, or otherwise without written permission from the publisher. It is illegal to copy this book, post it to a website, or distribute it by any other means without permission.

Brian Johnston asserts the moral right to be identified as the author of this work.

All scriptures, unless otherwise stated, are from the Scripture taken from the NASB NEW AMERICAN STANDARD BIBLE®, Copyright ©1960,1962,1963,1968,1971,1972,1973,1975,1977,1995 by The Lockman Foundation. Used by permission.

Scriptures marked NIV are from the THE HOLY BIBLE, NEW INTERNATIONAL VERSION® NIV® Copyright © 1973, 1978, 1984, 2011 by International Bible Society®. Used by permission. All rights reserved worldwide.

First edition

This book was professionally typeset on Reedsy. Find out more at reedsy.com

Contents

I THE CALL OF THE GOSPEL

1	THE CONTEXT OF THE GOSPEL - A CALL TO UNDERSTANDING THE...	3
2	THE CHANNEL OF THE GOSPEL - A CALL TO PERSONAL HOLINESS	9
3	THE CONTENT OF THE GOSPEL - A CALL TO BIBLICAL ORTHODOXY	15
4	THE COMMUNICATION OF THE GOSPEL - A CALL TO AUTHENTIC...	21

II THE LIGHT OF THE KNOWLEDGE OF THE GLORY OF GOD

5	.... IN THE ACT OF CREATION	29
6	... IN THE ACT OF GIVING THE LAW	36
7	... IN THE GLORY OF THE SAVIOUR	42
8	... IN THE GLORY OF THE SPIRIT'S WORKING IN BELIEVERS	47

III HAVING A LEG TO STAND ON IN THE GOD DEBATE

9	CREATION	55
10	CONSCIENCE	61
11	COMMUNICATION	67
12	CHRIST	72

IV USING PICTURES OF SALVATION

13	SLAVERY TO SIN – THE SLAVE MARKET (REDEMPTION)	81
14	SENTENCED TO DEATH – THE LAW COURTS (JUSTIFICATION)	86
15	UNDER GOD'S WRATH – THE TEMPLE SHRINE (PROPITIATION)	91
16	ALIENATED FROM GOD – THE FAMILY CIRCLE (RECONCILIATION)	96

ABOUT THE AUTHOR 101
MORE BOOKS FROM BRIAN JOHNSTON 102
ABOUT HAYES PRESS 105

I

THE CALL OF THE GOSPEL

As Christians we are called to preach the gospel, and to be effective when working in hard soil, we must heed the call to understand the times, be personally holy, ensure our message is Biblically accurate, and be sure to engage in evangelism authentically. This section explains why these 4 things are so important, and how to achieve them.

1

THE CONTEXT OF THE GOSPEL - A CALL TO UNDERSTANDING THE TIMES

There's a big difference between the Jewish audiences Paul often addressed in synagogues, and the group of Gentile philosophers he encountered at Athens. The Jews already had made their minds up. They thought they knew what the truth was, and they were only listening to see if Paul was teaching something different.

While the Gentile audience at Athens was searching for new opinions, it wasn't really all that keen to arrive at the truth. For them, the search was more enjoyable than embracing truth. Someone has said that the philosophers of Paul's day were to the truth what many co-habiting couples today are to marriage - they want to enjoy its pleasures, but also want to avoid its commitments and obligations. In other words, the Athenians liked to 'window shop' in the marketplace of truth, without buying.

Paul begins by telling this group that the God of whom he is speaking is the 'god' who was still unknown to them, but to whose existence an altar of theirs gave testimony (for it was marked as the altar 'to the unknown god'). Today, Nature is the unknown god. We hear statements like, 'it's nature's way of doing things' as if that explains why things are the way they are. And where did Nature come from? Ah, don't ask! Nature is the unknown 'god-of-the-gaps' for all those who reject the Bible's revelation.

It's instructive to compare Acts chapter 2 with Acts chapter 17. In Acts 2, we see Peter speaking at Jerusalem, to Jews or wannabe Jews. In that sermon, Peter uses the Old Testament Law to bring conviction (v.23), sounds a call to repentance (v.38), and the result of this open-air preaching was a massive three thousand conversions. Now let's look at Acts 17. Once again, we have an open-air sermon, this time delivered by Paul, but, remember, instead of addressing Jews, he's speaking to a group of Greeks in Athens (v.22). Like Peter, Paul also preaches sin and judgment (vv.30-31), but with a different outcome: some mocked, some wanted to hear more, and only a few believed.

There's such a marked difference between both the content and the outcome of these two sermons. Peter is speaking to Jews with a biblical foundation. To them the problem is Christ. But for the Greeks there's no foundation, no grounding in the Old Testament narrative, and Paul makes brief cultural references. For them the preaching of the cross is foolishness. In the western world, we're no longer a Christian society but much more like what Greek society was like back then. When presenting Christianity, we need to be prepared to give an answer to attacks made on the authority of Scripture. And we can't simply preach 'believe in Jesus' to biblically illiterate people who've no real idea of who Jesus is, much less any idea why he died on a cross. We live in an Acts 17-type society, and our preaching, to begin with, needs to help it to understand sin, and our accountability to the God who made us. The old idea that people already know they're sinners - and what sin is - is wrong. We must speak to the conscience of the person. Perhaps, it's worth asking: how did it come to be like this?

During the 14th to 16th centuries, in Europe, there was a movement known as the Renaissance. As the name suggests it was a revival of interest in literature generally, and this included the study of the Bible in its original languages and as translated into European languages such as German and English. It was a time when all kinds of learning flourished, and it was the time when the foundations of modern science were laid too. And there was a definite connection between scientific progress and the renewed interest in the Bible at that time. The return to the literal approach to biblical truth at this time fuelled advances in science. God-fearing scientists looked for law in nature because of their belief in a Law-giver: he being the Bible's author. When they found that law in nature, modern science was born.

But the 'Renaissance' was followed by the so-called 'Enlightenment' of the 17th to 19th centuries. In 1785, Scottish geologist James Hutton ruled out of court biblical explanations for the history of our planet. He decided, as a given, that the present must be key to the past. That was how the eighteenth century ended, and things were to get no better in the nineteenth. In the first half of the 19th century, an attitude to the Bible, known as 'higher criticism,' swept through German universities, spreading doubts about the Bible. This was an approach, a way of thinking, that questioned the Bible's authority. It opened the door for what was to follow in the second half of the 19th century. Godless evolutionary speculation built on this scepticism. In 1859, Darwin's Origin of Species, rewrote biblical history as not being 'his story' – that's God's story - but simply our own accidental and improbable arrival. In 1900 the German philosopher, Nietzsche, died but only after first having declared God to have predeceased him – God was dead, he said, as a philosophical idea. It was no coincidence that the 20th century that followed became the bloodiest in modern times, because accountability to any supernatural authority was set aside, with the framework for morality all but dismantled.

This decline of the West parallels the decline of society at the end of the glory days of the Roman Empire. We get a sense of what society was like then from Paul's letter to Rome:

> "For the wrath of God is revealed from heaven against all ungodliness and unrighteousness of men who suppress the truth in unrighteousness, because that which is known about God is evident within them; for God made it evident to them. For since the creation of the world His invisible attributes, His eternal power and divine nature, have been clearly seen, being understood through what has been made, so that they are without excuse. For even though they knew God, they did not honor Him as God or give thanks, but they became futile in their speculations, and their foolish heart was darkened. Professing to be wise, they became fools, and exchanged the glory of the incorruptible God for an image in the form of corruptible man and of birds and four-footed animals and crawling creatures. Therefore God gave them over in the lusts of their hearts to impurity, so that their bodies would be dishonored among them.
>
> For they exchanged the truth of God for a lie, and worshiped and served the creature rather than the Creator, who is blessed forever. Amen. For this reason God gave them over to degrading passions; for their women exchanged the natural function for that which is unnatural, and in the same way

also the men abandoned the natural function of the woman and burned in their desire toward one another, men with men committing indecent acts and receiving in their own persons the due penalty of their error. And just as they did not see fit to acknowledge God any longer, God gave them over to a depraved mind, to do those things which are not proper, being filled with all unrighteousness, wickedness, greed, evil; full of envy, murder, strife, deceit, malice; they are gossips, slanderers, haters of God, insolent, arrogant, boastful, inventors of evil, disobedient to parents, without understanding, untrustworthy, unloving, unmerciful; and although they know the ordinance of God, that those who practice such things are worthy of death, they not only do the same, but also give hearty approval to those who practice them" (Romans 1:18-32).

Quite an indictment of society, isn't it? These could be today's newspaper headlines. Richard Holloway, professor of divinity, wrote an article published in the Scotsman newspaper on Wednesday 13 November, 2019, in which he presumed to address the author of Genesis, and said: 'you went on to craft a great poem describing how God made everything in six days and rested on the seventh. That's where the trouble started ... some people started to read you, not as a glorious fiction that prompted their wonder, but as an accurate news report of a tumultuous week about six thousand years ago.'

When religious leaders stopped viewing Genesis as historical, and when the Judeo-Christian foundations of western society were eroded by anti-biblical thinking, our society – like the society the Apostle Paul describes in Romans chapter 1 - entered into its moral decline because people abandoned the ethical implications of being made in God's image. It's the book of Genesis that defines who we are as human beings, made by God as male and female. This fundamental truth is being reinterpreted today to serve the latest fashion and thinking. Redefining basic biological reality is foolhardy. Marriage is clearly defined in Genesis as a life-long union being between one man and one woman. However, some people – like the author we quoted – take to themselves the liberty to re-define this sacred institution. We need make no mistake, our society is well down the same road as the first century society which the Apostle Paul wrote about in his Bible letter to Rome. The decline of the West parallels the decline of society in the fading glory of the Roman Empire. This is what inevitably happens when we stop reading Genesis correctly: when we stop reading it according to the rules of literature.

When an American evangelist was recently banned from a venue in Glasgow, a Church of Scotland minister said Scottish Christians were not comfortable with the fact that the evangelist in question was opposed to same-sex marriage. Religious leaders have no business apologizing for having stated that the proper place for sexual activity is within a marriage between a man and a woman. To say that is to say what the Bible says. Let's conclude this with a little known fact: more that 60% of all Nobel prize winners between 1900 and 2000 were those who professed belief in God. One of them put it like this: "what science has now discovered is what we might expect based on the Book of Genesis."

2

THE CHANNEL OF THE GOSPEL - A CALL TO PERSONAL HOLINESS

In parts of the world, speaking God's Word in public spaces still draws crowds. Showing an introductory film and some singing does help to thicken the crowd, but these listeners remain throughout the whole time when the message is preached. Often there's a response, sometimes sizable, and the number added to the local church demonstrates the reality of that response, at least in part. For the preacher concerned, there are few experiences to compare with an evening in a remote village under the stars when there comes a moment during the delivery of the message when the audience is no longer restless: a stillness falls over them, and there could well be a tear in the eyes of those close enough to be visible. Occasionally, heads begin to bow. The speaker senses God at work, the Spirit touching hearts, sensitizing them to sin, and with mounting anticipation, he prepares to call for a verdict ...

It's normally a different experience in the western world, isn't it? Are we nowadays, I wonder, more often concerned with numbers populating our pre-evangelistic activities than with expectantly testifying to the glory of the Gospel of Christ? Rather than devoting a lot of time to innovations, the preacher will make private communion with God a top priority. The Word of God, and time spent in God's presence, is the means the Holy Spirit uses to transform us into the image of Christ. 'If the Word does not dwell in us with power' wrote Puritan John Owen, 'it will not pass from us with power' (*The Works of John Owen*, vol. 16, p. 76.). If our evangelism is to be effective, meditation with God over his Word must be more important to us than discovering the latest way to attract crowds. Because, if we think about it, it must be hard for the average unchurched person to figure out why a group of people supposedly filled with God's Spirit, and able to speak with the Creator of the universe, would need to resort to using gimmicks.

In the nineteenth chapter of Matthew's gospel, Jesus tells a rich young ruler the realities of true discipleship. As the rich man realized that personal sacrifice is required to live in God's kingdom, he walked away. Jesus didn't run after the man in an effort to make the Gospel more appealing. No, Jesus let him go, because the only terms on which anyone can really follow Christ are God's own terms.

Francis Chan tells a modern parable when he says: Suppose I was concerned about people's health so I ... rented a building and painted a cool sign with a bunch of happy vegetables on it. I began making drinks by blending kale, carrots, beets, and spinach. My customers loved my drinks and came daily. There was just one problem: there aren't enough health fanatics to keep my business afloat. My solution: whipped cream. Once I topped my drinks with it, more people started coming around. Soon after, I added chocolate syrup and sales grew even more. Once gummy bears and M&M's were introduced, I started making a fortune. I would still boast that my drinks contained some healthy ingredients, even though I knew my clients were getting fatter and more lethargic.

My desire to run a lucrative business at some point overpowered my original goal of health. At some point in the process, I should have taken down the sign. Prayer, Communion, fellowship, and Bible reading don't attract large crowds. So we start adding elements that will attract people. We accomplish a goal, but it is the wrong goal. (Letters to the Church (pp. 96-97). David C Cook. Kindle Edition.)

He's got a point, hasn't he? The earliest believers didn't try to do lots of activities, but instead they devoted themselves to a few. The Apostles' motto was 'prayer and the ministry of the Word.' The priorities of those very first believers were: prayer (Acts 4); the Word (Acts 6); witnessing (Acts 3-5); having confidence in a God who could do beyond the ordinary (Acts 3-5); and embracing whatever hardship was necessary for God's work to progress (Acts 3-5). While they gave themselves to these things, Acts 2:43 tells us "everyone kept feeling a sense of awe." Can we experience biblical awe without biblical devotion?

In Old Testament history, the Israelites had known deliverance from slavery in Egypt; they had the law of God; they'd experienced the provision of all their needs in the desert; they had the building plan for God's house to be among them; and they were heading to a promised land flowing with milk and honey. But Moses says that even all that isn't enough without God's accompanying presence (Exodus 33:2,3,15-19).

And we've got all their blessings available to us today in a spiritual form, as well as the assurance of the indwelling Spirit of God, but do we also – as Moses did - long for a greater sense of God's presence as we make the claim to live in God's living quarters on earth? In our worship, do we have a palpable sense of: entering the holy place above in full assurance of faith, seeing him who is invisible, and making contact with ultimate reality? Entering the holies is to experience the presence of God. Turning to our witness, we long for more repetitions of that moment of spiritual tension we described earlier when victory is sensed in preaching and tokens of repentance are detected among the audience. In our daily Christian walk, we hunger for being more often aware of things happening for which there can be no other explanation than the Lord has drawn near and shown his hand in the everyday.

We try to attract people in different ways, but what if we presented ourselves as people with an inexpressible joy, with a peace that surpasses comprehension, and with the availability of an immeasurably great power? How could they then fail to be intrigued - if we were people committed to worshipping God, people who can't get enough of time in his presence - where it's the object of our worship and not the atmosphere that makes worshipping exciting to us? And the goal is not merely to tolerate each other but to actually love one another to the same extent that Christ loved us, and to be united in God to the same extent that the Father is one with the Son (John 17:21); a community where no-one is a mere consumer, but each is a gifted contributor. We want to be people with something not of this world about us, regularly sharing the gospel with neighbours and co-workers, far from seeking comfort, a people thriving on hardship, refusing to become citizens of this earth.

Sometimes we hear people say they enjoyed a spiritual high when in the company of hundreds of their contemporaries at some big event where their favourite worship music was being played. But I'd have to say that some of the most poignant times I've known, when I've most sensed the presence of God, have been with relatively few folks who are there for no other reason than their devotion to spending time with God. It's not about who else may or may not be present. We could sometimes say, 'God, look how many people are coming because they love being with you!' But God knows exactly how many would be there if there was no special program, only prayer and Bible teaching. Paul actually told Timothy that teaching sound doctrine will not 'work' – that is, it'll not bring in the crowds; in fact, it'll do the opposite (2 Timothy 4:1–5). But Paul didn't change the menu because of that. Timothy was commanded to preach truth simply because it's what God wants! And that's what matters, provided, of course, it's presented in a contemporary – but undiluted - way that connects with the audience and engages with the culture.

Imagine you go to a restaurant and order a fillet steak. Thirty minutes later, the waiter returns and puts a pizza in front of you, claiming it's the best pizza you'll ever try. What would you do? I'm pretty sure you'd send it back - because it wasn't what you ordered, not even close. Well, God gave us his 'order' – I mean, he told us exactly how he wanted to be served through his commandments in the New Testament, but instead of us delivering exactly what he asked for, we got distracted by thinking about what we want and what others seem to want, and by what's been done traditionally by the generations before us.

How can we make progress? Well, that's the theme of the briefing Paul gives to Timothy. Let's come back to our preacher, a man captivated by the presence of God, aware that nothing counts apart from God. He's a man of prayer, and prayer implies that all our gifts and efforts are very much the dispensable part. The Apostle Paul's briefing of Timothy, the preacher, went like this: "Be an example," he told him (1 Timothy 4:12) for starters. We have to practice what we preach. While stationed in Scotland, Colonel Durnford happened to be between Berwick and Holy Island, where a small craft had stuck on the coast during a storm. Seeing the hesitation of the fishermen to go to the rescue, he jumped into a boat, calling out, 'Will none of you come with me? If not, I shall go alone.' A volunteer crew at once joined him and succeeded in rescuing those in peril. That's the power of example.

Next, Paul told Timothy to give attention to reading (1 Timothy 4:13). Certainly, the public reading of the Bible, but that must be based on unremitting Bible study by the preacher. It was said of some of the old mines of Cornwall that the deeper they were sunk the richer they proved to be; and though some lodes had been followed a thousand, and even fifteen hundred, feet, they'd not come to an end. Bible study is like that. The Bible is a mine of wealth which can never be exhausted. The deeper we sink into it the richer it becomes "Don't neglect your gift," Paul added (1 Timothy 4:14). Later, it's represented as a living fire which must be cared for; a spark of the Spirit, likely to smoulder if neglected, and needing to be blown into flame by vigorous exercise.

Then he says, "Be diligent" (1 Timothy 4:15) or, more bluntly put, don't be lazy. Any endowment we have by the grace of God is no excuse for mental laziness. The study of the Word of God involves constant reading, research, and intense thought. It's the highest field of study and research, albeit under God's Spirit and through prayer. All our faculties need to be engaged. The preacher needs to ring-fence his preparation time when he's standing in God's council. Paul's final point is about the need of the messenger to pay attention to himself (1 Timothy 4:16). An actor may utter a word that touches the heart, but the messenger of the gospel must personally know the truths he proclaims to others. The power of preaching depends upon a constant sense of the reality and solemnity of eternal truths.

3

THE CONTENT OF THE GOSPEL - A CALL TO BIBLICAL ORTHODOXY

There are many distortions of the Gospel today. The Gospel, of course, means Good News, and it's the good news about how we can be free from the claims of God's justice and spend eternity in his presence. It's about what God has done for us, supremely through his son and through the cross. The false notions or distortions of the Gospel, that we were referring to, tend to be of a sort that tries to turn the Gospel into a human-centred Gospel.

For example, such a false Gospel may proclaim that we humans are not so bad: that we are at least capable of believing all by ourselves. And the popular view of ourselves as masters of our own destiny, tends to play to the idea of everyone – without any outside influence being brought to bear – being capable of making their own decision one way or another, with our personal decision being a decision that God anticipates and merely honours. And another common distortion is the claim that it's our duty to do enough good things later so as to keep hold of that status of being acceptable before God.

These may not seem to be major distortions – at least not compared to the so-called 'Prosperity Gospel' that tells us that God wants us to be wealthy and healthy in this world, and it's down to our lack of faith if we're not – but they're still very significant distortions. I want us to see why such things as we mentioned a moment ago, are serious distortions of the Gospel of God. The fundamental difference is they make the Gospel more human-centred than God-centred. In fact, the Gospel is not only God-centred, but it's Trinity-centred. Let's take a reading from 1 Corinthians 2:1-4:

> "And when I came to you, brethren, I did not come with superiority of speech or of wisdom, proclaiming to you the testimony of God. For I determined to know nothing among you except Jesus Christ, and Him crucified. I was with you in weakness and in fear and in much trembling, and my message and my preaching were not in persuasive words of wisdom, but in demonstration of the Spirit and of power, so that your faith would not rest on the wisdom of men, but on the power of God."

Notice there the Apostle Paul describes the Gospel he was proclaiming as "the testimony of God" and it was about "Christ, and Him crucified," delivered in "the demonstration of the Spirit." There's mention of Father, Son and Spirit, all in connection with the Gospel. In fact, the so-called 'church father,' Basil the Great, is reputed to have originated the saying that goes like this: 'everything that God does comes from the Father in the Son through the Spirit'. That statement finds strong support from the Bible. We're focusing on the Gospel here, so let's investigate what the New Testament actually tells us about the Gospel.

It tells us that the Father in eternity gave the Son people whom the Spirit would eventually join to him in history (2 Thessalonians 2:13; Ephesians 1:13). Jesus very clearly says this in his John 17 prayer. In verse 9, Jesus clarifies that the prayer he's offering is not "on behalf of the world, but of those whom You have given Me," he says to his Father. This is an idea repeated many times in Christ's prayer, that both his prayer and work is on behalf of those whom the Father has given to him, not everyone. This agrees with what is disclosed to us as we begin reading Paul's letter to the Ephesians. In the counsels of eternity, the Son joyfully signed his own death warrant, meaning that one day as the man Christ Jesus, he would go to the cross and die. It was all planned.

Not only were we (believers) chosen in Christ "before the foundation of the world" (Ephesians 1:4), but Christ himself is described as the Lamb slain from the foundation of the world, as John adds in the Book of Revelation (Revelation 13:8). Don't we begin to see how God-centred the Gospel is? And never more so than at the cross. The Old Testament prophet, Zechariah says in chapter 12, "In that day," declares the LORD, "I will pour out on the house of David and on the inhabitants of Jerusalem, the Spirit of grace and of supplication, so that they will look on Me whom they have pierced ..."

Please observe that it's the LORD (God) who says he has been pierced. And compare now what we find in the very next chapter, Zechariah chapter 13 and verse 7: '"Awake, O sword, against My Shepherd, And against the man, My Associate,' declares the LORD of hosts. 'Strike the Shepherd that the sheep may be scattered.'" Please also observe that it's once again the LORD (in capitals as it's not a mere title but the name of God, as Yahweh) who is the one wielding or directing the sword of divine justice. Isn't this the deep, impenetrable mystery of the cross? It's the Word become flesh (John 1:14), the second person of the Trinity, robed in mortal flesh who has been pierced and who died on the cross. But equally do those texts from Zechariah not show that it was the LORD (God – same name) who was responsible for the piercing also? This is God, in our nature, struck and pierced by God – this occurring within a triune God in which the second person was robed with mortal flesh. All this to demonstrate his righteousness and uphold perfect divine justice while granting forgiveness to each repentant believer. This is the awesome wonder of the God-centred Gospel!

Returning to where we were a moment ago, Jesus more than once in John's Gospel speaks of people having been given to him by the Father, starting in John chapter 6 (John 6:39; 10:29; 17:2, 6–10). They're called and kept by the Holy Spirit for the consummation of the new creation (Romans 8:29–30; Ephesians 1:11–13; Titus 3:5; 1 Peter 1:5). Must this not show that Christ's death was – and remains – effective for all for whom it was intended to be effective? Let's steer clear of any hint of a human-centred Gospel – one that says Christ was sent on a venture that was to any extent uncertain as to who might or might not be saved. But someone might say: 'Don't the Scriptures talk of God's purposes reaching to all peoples?' Quite so, and this needed to be stressed in New Testament times for we know how the Jews supposed salvation was only for themselves; hence the emphatic - but sometimes equivocal – use of the words 'all' and 'the world' to show God's planned extension to Gentiles. In God's plan, salvation was never going to be limited to Jews.

But a human-centred Gospel tends to lead in thought towards universalism. The first letter of John chapter 2, and verse 1, has been misused in this connection. Here the translation and interpretation of Christ making propitiation for the sins of the world leads readily to the idea of universalism. But 'universalism' – the salvation of literally all - is totally untenable. Speaking very definitely of certain persons, Jesus said in Matthew 25:46, "These will go away into eternal punishment, but the righteous into eternal life," and so "the whole world" as the Apostle John uses it, cannot imply absolutely everyone's sins were dealt with, but only again indicates that those whom God most definitely intended to be saved were not confined to the Jewish nation (as was the typical mindset back then).

Not only is God's sovereignty and freedom in electing grace seen, but the Trinitarian character of that divine purpose is also seen. For it all takes place "in Christ" (Ephesians 3:11); yet, it's not only Christ-centred but Trinity-centred, as we saw from 1 Corinthians 2:1-5 earlier. The Christian faith is distinguished by its claim that God is the Father, the Son, and the Holy Spirit, and we know this straight from the Bible, for example from the Apostle John's writings when he says the Word entered into a fallen world in our own flesh (John 1:14), as sent by the Father (1 John 4:9), and having the Spirit, in his anointing, upon him (John 1:32).

Not only is the Trinitarian character of God's purpose in salvation seen in his electing grace, but a Trinitarian understanding of the gospel clears up a lot of other popular misunderstandings. For example, it challenges presentations of the Gospel that make it sound as if our Lord became the 'whipping-boy' for the Father's anger. Far from it, the Father sent and gave his Son so that all believers will never perish (1 John 4:9,10,14). It was the Father who chose us in Christ before the foundation of the world (Ephesians 1:4); it was the Son who gave himself up for us (Galatians 2:20) – and this as a willing sacrifice: "No one takes [my life] from me," he said. "I have authority to lay it down, and I have authority to take it up again" (John 4:34; 10:11, 18). He went to the cross knowing that his suffering would lead to glory not only for him but for those his Father had given to him (Hebrews 2:10).

The Spirit's work is to lift the veil that rests on human hearts and blinds them to the Gospel (2 Corinthians 3:16; 4:4). All are spiritually dead (Ephesians 2:1) and so totally unresponsive until he awakens them, at once convicting of sin (John 16:8) and regenerating to new life (John 3:3-5; Titus 3:5). Without the Spirit's influence on a person's life, no-one can receive Christ. Let's thank God for this God-centred Good News that's from the Father, in the Son, and through the Spirit – a Gospel that brings salvation to all whom God intended.

4

THE COMMUNICATION OF THE GOSPEL - A CALL TO AUTHENTIC EVANGELISM

There's a rich vocabulary used to describe the Apostle Paul's preaching activity at Thessalonica. It's variously said that he reasoned; he explained; he gave evidence; he proclaimed; and he persuaded. Despite his conviction that evangelism was underwritten by God's sovereignty, Paul's energetic performance is certainly on display here. He definitely was someone who preached for a verdict every time.

But he wasn't without his critics – both then and now. Why now? Well, Paul's been criticized for apparently not opening his Bible and preaching the cross graphically to the Athenians as he did to the Galatians (Galatians 3:1) or for not confining himself exclusively to Christ and him crucified as per his remarks to the Corinthians (1 Corinthians 2:2). However, as we've commented in an earlier study, this criticism totally overlooks the fact that Paul was delivering this sermon to an audience who didn't have any biblical foundation whatsoever. Paul begins by telling this group that the God of whom he is speaking is the 'god' who was unknown to them, but to whose existence an altar of theirs gave testimony. Today, Nature is the unknown god. We hear statements like, 'it's nature's way of doing things' as if that explains why things are the way they are.

It's instructive to compare Acts 2 with Acts 17. In Acts 2, we see Peter speaking at Jerusalem, to Jews or wannabe Jews. In these verses, Peter uses the Old Testament Law to bring conviction (v.23), sounds a call to repentance (v.38); and the result of this open-air sermon was a massive three thousand conversions. Now let's look at Acts 17. Once again, we have an open-air sermon, this time delivered by Paul. Instead of addressing Jews, he's speaking to a group of Greeks in Athens (v.22). Like Peter, Paul also preaches of sin and judgment (vv.30-31), but with a different outcome: some mocked, some wanted to hear more, and only a few believed.

Interestingly, it's Peter (1 Peter 3:15) who gives us the text usually referenced by those engaging in apologetics. Apologetics is the approach that meets people where they are, and engages with their existing worldview. It aims to show the other person we've understood their framework of beliefs, and gently moves on to encourage them to doubt it or otherwise see its inconsistency, before showing how the Christian worldview better addresses their own concerns, for example about morality or justice or the meaning of life or where we've come from. The Judeo-Christian biblical worldview is the only one that comes up with coherent answers.

It's equally important to acknowledge that apologetics is a door-opener, it's first base only. But let's not assume we can omit it. The Apostle Paul was right to use this approach with the Athenians, and the same would apply to us in the west now. And the apologetic most needed now in the west is an apologetic for the existence of God. So then, how does Paul begin? It's by saying:

> "The God who made the world and all things in it, since He is Lord of heaven and earth, does not dwell in temples made with hands; nor is He served by human hands, as though He needed anything, since He Himself gives to all people life and breath and all things..." (Acts 17:24-25).

In other words, he makes the case for the existence of a creator. Materialism is not the answer. It is widely recognized that there has to be more than mass and energy. Einstein said he could identify no means by which matter could give meaning to symbols. The clear implication is that symbolic information, or language, represents a category of reality distinct from matter and energy. In this way, Einstein pointed to the nature and origin of symbolic information as one of the profound questions about the world. That means there are, in fact, three fundamental quantities: mass, energy and also information. The DNA code of all life-forms is an example of information, which, like any other information, cannot arise from anything material, but requires an intelligent sender. This is supernatural intelligence whom the Bible introduces to us as the Judeo-Christian God.

Having pointed to God's existence, Paul moved on to the origins of humanity: "and He made from one man every nation of mankind to live on all the face of the earth, having determined their appointed times and the boundaries of their habitation" (Acts 17:26). We've all seen the iconic graphic showing progressively more upright (hominid / apemen) species between ape and humans. Here's a reality check on that: it's impossible for us to categorically determine species from fossils because obviously there's no way we can observe how fossils either can or can't interbreed (which is the way we define what all belongs to the same species)! Extinct ape fossils may share characteristics with modern humans, but so do living apes. Nothing directly supports a transition from ape to human. The plain implication of Paul's words – not to mention any plain reading of biblical texts – is people have always been people and apes have always been apes (1 Corinthians 15:39). Each created according to the purpose and plan of God.

Having accounted for origins in his worldview, Paul now moves on to meaning and purpose: "that they would seek God, if perhaps they might grope for Him and find Him, though He is not far from each one of us" (Acts 17:27). Paul references the search for something beyond ourselves. Beautiful objects may distract us, and even content us for a while, but the experience of countless lives is that material things don't ultimately satisfy us. That's what the Rolling Stones were intending to say when they mangled the grammar, and said 'I can't find no satisfaction.' Author C.S. Lewis put it in a more literary form when he said: "Creatures are not born with desires unless satisfaction for these desires exists. A baby feels hunger; well, there is such a thing as food ... If I find in myself a desire which no experience in this world can satisfy, the most probable explanation is that I was made for another world" (Mere Christianity, Bk. III, chap. 10, "Hope").

Someone (Peter Kreeft) has used that as another argument for God's existence: every natural, innate desire in us corresponds to some real object that can satisfy that desire. But there exists in us a desire which nothing in time, nothing on earth, and no creature can satisfy. Therefore, there must exist something more than time, earth, and creatures, which can satisfy this desire. This something is what people call 'God' and 'life with God forever.' We would readily recognize desires we all have, such as: to be appreciated, to have happiness, to find fulfilment, but ultimately only a relationship with God offers these in fullest measure.

The French philosopher effectively wrote about us all having a God-shaped hole (Blaise Pascal, *Pensées* VII(425)). In other words, we have desires that nothing material can satisfy because we were designed for fellowship with God, having been created in his image.

In the prevailing pagan culture of that time and place, Paul felt the need to stress he was not talking about man-made or any created gods. What he next said was this: "Being then the children of God, we ought not to think that the Divine Nature is like gold or silver or stone, an image formed by the art and thought of man" (Acts 17:29). A lady in my church was telling me that while she'd been witnessing to her son, he'd turned around and asked her: 'And who made God?' At first hearing, that question might seem a stunner, but then we realize it's simply an ill-defined question. We might compare it with the other ill-defined question of our age: 'How long is a piece of string?' In a similar way, there's no answer to that, but that doesn't mean any specific string has no length, far less does it mean that there is no such thing as string!

Well, Paul is drawing to a conclusion now. And remember we said apologetics is not enough on its own. It simply sets the stage, and gains us a hearing. So, let's hear from Paul: "Therefore having overlooked the times of ignorance, God is now declaring to men that all people everywhere should repent, because He has fixed a day in which He will judge the world in righteousness through a Man whom He has appointed, having furnished proof to all men by raising Him from the dead" (Acts 17:30-31).

May I ask you whether you believe that moral wrongs should be punished? If the answer is yes, then it really requires an afterlife for those who escape justice here. And now a follow-up question: 'Have you ever done any wrongs?' That makes it personal, doesn't it? Life's inequalities demand ultimate justice, and how will we, personally, fare? One man ranting about the evils of the world was asked: 'and what about the evil you see within your own heart?' Forgiveness becomes a relevant issue. Where else has it been made available to humans other than in the death and resurrection of Jesus Christ, whom Paul referred to here? Charles Colson, special counsel to US President Nixon said: "I know the resurrection is a fact, and Watergate proved it to me. How? Because 12 men testified they had seen Jesus raised from the dead, then they proclaimed that truth for 40 years, never once denying it. Every one was beaten, tortured, stoned and put in prison. They would not have endured that if it weren't true. Watergate embroiled 12 of the most powerful men in the world – and they couldn't keep a lie for three weeks. You're telling me 12 apostles could keep a lie for 40 years? Absolutely impossible." Jesus truly did rise, showing he was who he claimed to be. No resurrection, then no Christianity … and no hope.

II

THE LIGHT OF THE KNOWLEDGE OF THE GLORY OF GOD

Sowing the gospel in hard soil can be a challenging experience, and even the Apostle Paul found it so. It is good to be reminded, then, of the glorious reality of the gospel that we are preaching and the Saviour who is the focus of that message. In this section, we look at 4 things in which God's glory is clearly seen – in the act of creation, the act of giving the Law, the act of giving His Son, and the act of giving the Holy Spirit.

5

.... IN THE ACT OF CREATION

On a few occasions in the New Testament, the Apostle Paul urges his readers not to lose heart. In particular, he appeals that they don't lose heart in evangelism. This appeal can be found – twice in fact - in Second Corinthians chapter 4. And if we're in the western world today, it's not hard to appreciate why he had this concern about people losing heart. Paul encountered in certain places the same stony indifference we can come up against, ranging even to outright hostility at times. We can all too readily identify the same features in society around us that the Apostle Paul diagnoses in the Greco-Roman world of the first century AD (Romans 1). And we recall that it was in places such as Capernaum that our Lord could do no mighty work – that is, rather, he chose not to – due to their lack of faith.

The German philosopher, Nietzsche, who died in the year 1900, is the person most famed for popularizing the notion that God was dead. In other words, the age of faith in a deity who was our maker and judge was over, he said. Darwin had by then recently made it possible for people to believe there was no God, only time and chance. And if that was true, then it followed that we could just make up our own rules. Nietzsche understood that such an idea – as with any idea – had consequences. With the framework of absolute truth and morality dismantled, he foresaw the horrors that awaited the world in the twentieth century: those being the bloodiest in recorded history. He realized the atheist dream was unliveable, turning the world into an Auschwitz. He personally died a madman, and it was as if he'd even predicted this fate, for he famously wrote:

"The madman jumped into their midst and pierced them with his eyes. 'Whither is God,' he cried; 'I will tell you. *We have killed him* - you and I! All of us are his murderers ... Do we not feel the breath of empty space? Has it not become colder? ... Do we smell nothing as yet of the divine decomposition? Gods, too, decompose. God is dead. God remains dead. And we have killed him.'"

Nietzsche's atheism, unlike many contemporary atheistic mantras, was not simply rhetoric and angry words. He recognized that the death of God introduced a significant crisis. He understood the critical role of the Christian story to the very underpinnings of European philosophy, history, and culture, and so understood that God's death meant that a total—and painful—transformation of reality had to take place. If God has died in the sense that God is no longer of any use to us, then ours is a world in peril, he reasoned, for *everything must change.* Our typical way of thought and life no longer makes sense; the structures for evaluating everything have become unhinged. He spoke of erasing the horizon, and no longer knowing which was north and which was south.

This delusion still permeates much of western society today. And it is a delusion, make no mistake about it. Listen to how the Apostle Paul will come to talk about society having been blinded, or in other words, deluded. But we'll start a little further back in his writing in

Second Corinthians chapter 3. Here he begins by contrasting the Law of Moses, and its famous Ten Commandments, with Christianity and the supernatural empowerment it provides through the Holy Spirit given to believers by God. Let's listen to Paul:

> "But if the ministry of death, in letters engraved on stones, came with glory, so that the sons of Israel could not look intently at the face of Moses because of the glory of his face, fading as it was, how will the ministry of the Spirit fail to be even more with glory? For if the ministry of condemnation has glory, much more does the ministry of righteousness abound in glory. For indeed what had glory, in this case has no glory because of the glory that surpasses it. For if that which fades away was with glory, much more that which remains is in glory.
>
> Therefore having such a hope, we use great boldness in our speech, and are not like Moses, who used to put a veil over his face so that the sons of Israel would not look intently at the end of what was fading away. But their minds were hardened; for until this very day at the reading of the old covenant the same veil remains unlifted, because it is removed in Christ. But to this day whenever Moses is read, a veil lies over their heart; but whenever a person turns to the Lord, the veil is taken away. Now the Lord is the Spirit, and where the Spirit of the Lord is, there is liberty. But we all, with unveiled face, beholding as in a mirror the glory of the Lord, are being transformed into the same image from glory to glory, just as from the Lord, the Spirit" (2 Corinthians 3:7-18).

Let's pause there to appreciate the contrast Paul has just made. We are not like Moses, he says (v.13), in that Moses put a veil over his face. The difference, he says, is that we – the witnessing Christian believer – remain unveiled before others as we communicate God's Good News in Jesus Christ, both beholding God's glory and reflecting (or mirroring) it to others in an unveiled way. A Christian preacher first stands in the presence of God, at that point unveiled like Moses: but the preacher continues to remain unveiled - unlike Moses. However, there is still a veil – but it's now transferred to unbelieving hearts and minds, as Paul goes on to explain further:

> "Therefore, since we have this ministry, as we received mercy, we do not lose heart, but we have renounced the things hidden because of shame, not walking in craftiness or adulterating the word of God, but by the manifestation of truth commending ourselves to every man's conscience in the sight of God. And even if our gospel is veiled, it is veiled to those who are perishing, in whose case the god of this world has blinded the minds of the unbelieving so that they might not see the light of the gospel of the glory of Christ, who is the image of God. For we do not preach ourselves but Christ Jesus as Lord, and ourselves as your bond-servants for Jesus' sake. For God, who said, 'Light shall shine out of darkness,' is the One who has shone in our hearts to give the Light of the knowledge of the glory of God in the face of Christ. But we have this treasure in earthen vessels, so that the surpassing greatness of the power will be of God and not from ourselves" (2 Corinthians 4:1-7).

Yes, indeed, Satan blinds the unbelieving to the glory of the only saviour, who is Jesus Christ. Now, I want you to notice that we were reminded there of some of the first words found in the Bible. They concern God's working in creation when, in Genesis 1:3, God famously said "Let there be light." This was what we heard Paul saying a moment ago as we read from Second Corinthians chapter 4: "God, who said, 'Light shall shine out of darkness,' is the One who has shone in our hearts to give the Light of the knowledge of the glory of God in the face of Christ." God has not left himself without witness or evidence. Although the text references God creating and bringing light out of darkness in order to point to his fuller revelation of himself in Jesus Christ, I want to pause on the first part for now. I want us to think first of how it's possible to detect the light of the knowledge of the glory of God in the act of creation. The Bible testifies to the glory of the Creator.

A sceptical world demands evidence for the existence of God. We can begin right here with the universe around us. I know some illustrious names have lent credence to the idea of the universe somehow managing to create itself. But even those at the level of Philosophy 101 realise this can never withstand scrutiny at the most basic level we can all understand. There is a law, known as the Law of Non-Contradiction, and it doesn't allow for anything both to exist and not exist at the same time – no more than a door can be green and not be green at the same time. And a universe that's busy creating itself has somehow got to exist (so as to do the creating) and also not to exist (so as to be created). And that is nonsense.

Ah, but someone will sneer this doesn't apply to the mysterious world of matter and anti-matter which, when combined, give you nothing. And so just as easily, in reverse, you can get something out of nothing. Really? No, not really. This is smoke and mirrors, I'm afraid. This so-called 'nothing' is not nothing at all: it's a sea of energy obeying some special laws of physics – and that's not nothing! That play on the word 'nothing' is the same type of illusion as saying 'Margarine is better than nothing.' And also adding: 'Nothing is better than butter.' And then claiming you can put these two sentences together and reason that margarine is better than butter – when clearly you've been using the word 'nothing' in two different senses in these two sentences. It's smoke and mirrors. It's an illusion. It's a delusion to think any object – however small or large – can self-materialize or in other words can pop into existence unaided, all by itself.

We can say that like this:

1. If anything begins to exist, then it must have a cause. (Something else that makes it to exist).
2. The universe had a beginning. (We know that because things get more and more disordered with the passing of time, and we do not yet see all things as totally disordered, for the universe still functions).
3. Therefore, it follows, that the universe had a cause. (Something that caused it to exist.)

Let's put it yet another way. If you were walking along the beach and saw a perfectly formed capital letter 'A' scratched in the sand, what conclusion would you draw? Would you suppose that the random actions of the tides, winds and waves had dragged along some pebble or brushwood and randomly formed that letter? I doubt it. You'd much more likely assume someone whose name begins with the letter 'A' had left his or her mark. And that's just one letter. You don't need me to remind you that in every cell of our bodies, in the human genome, we have three billion letters that prescribe who we are – at least genetically. These are the gifts we receive from our parents in terms of DNA. The complexity of the human cell and of the marvellous information molecules of our DNA was sufficient to cause one renowned British atheist to renounce atheism. Very late in life, Antony Flew finally came to glimpse something of the light of the knowledge of the glory of God in creation – glory that's also declared by the heavens, the Bible says (Psalm 19:1)!

6

... IN THE ACT OF GIVING THE LAW

The German philosopher, Nietzsche, who died in the year 1900, is the person famed for popularizing the idea that God is dead. In other words, he proclaimed the age of faith in a deity who was our maker and judge was over. Darwin had then recently made it possible for people to believe there was no God, with only time and chance being responsible for all that we see. And if that was true, then it followed that we could make up our own rules. Nietzsche understood that such an idea – as with any idea – had consequences. With the framework of absolute truth and morality dismantled, he foresaw the horrors that awaited the world in the twentieth century: those being the bloodiest in recorded history.

And still we've not learnt our lesson. The delusion that there's no God still permeates western society. In a moment, we'll hear how the Apostle Paul talks about society having been blinded, or in other words, deluded. But let's start a little further back in his writings – writing that's found in Second Corinthians chapter 3. Here he begins by contrasting the Law of Moses with its famous Ten Commandments with Christianity and the supernatural empowerment it provides through the Holy Spirit given to believers by God. Let's listen to Paul:

> "But if the ministry of death, in letters engraved on stones, [that's referring to the Ten Commandments written on two stone tablets] came with glory, so that the sons of Israel could not look intently at the face of Moses because of the glory of his face, fading as it was, how will the ministry of the Spirit fail to be even more with glory? For if the ministry of condemnation has glory, much more does the ministry of righteousness abound in glory. For indeed what had glory, in this case has no glory because of the glory that surpasses it. For if that which fades away was with glory, much more that which remains is in glory.
>
> Therefore having such a hope, we use great boldness in our speech, and are not like Moses, who used to put a veil over his face so that the sons of Israel would not look intently at the end of what was fading away. But their minds were hardened; for until this very day at the reading of the old covenant the same veil remains unlifted, because it is removed in Christ. But to this day whenever Moses is read, a veil lies over their heart; but whenever a person turns to the Lord, the veil is taken away. Now the Lord is the Spirit, and where the Spirit of the Lord is, there is liberty. But we all, with unveiled face, beholding as in a mirror the glory of the Lord, are being transformed into the same image from glory to glory, just as from the Lord, the Spirit" (2 Corinthians 3:7-18).

Paul informs us here that there was a glory associated with the Law, with the giving of the Law through Moses to the Jewish people, God's people, in Old Testament times. He's referring to a visible glory. That wasn't the only glory, however. Moses could say to the people in his time: "... what great nation is there that has statutes and judgments as righteous as this whole law which I am setting before you today?" (Deuteronomy 4:8). In other words, there was also a moral glory that belonged to the Law. There was a virtue and a value in that moral code God gave to Israel that no other people on earth had. It's testimony to this value that the justice systems of many western lands were built basically upon the principles that are enshrined in God's Law with its Ten Commandments. But this wonderful legacy of Judeo-Christian influence is now being increasingly eroded in western society.

But let's get back to the fact that the Apostle Paul was really talking about a visible glory associated with the giving of the Law at the time of Moses. When Moses came out from the presence of God the skin of his face shone. However, the effect faded over time. To prevent the people from being able to see the radiance of his face decreasing, Moses, we're told, used to place a veil over his face. Then Paul says something quite striking. He tells us that we're not like Moses. The difference, he says, is that we – meaning witnessing Christian believers today – remain physically unveiled before others whenever we communicate God's Good News in Jesus Christ. But that doesn't mean there's no veil of any kind today. There is, Paul says, only it's now transferred to the unbelieving hearts of listeners. Paul goes on to explain:

> "Therefore, since we have this ministry, as we received mercy, we do not lose heart, but we have renounced the things hidden because of shame, not walking in craftiness or adulterating the word of God, but by the manifestation of truth commending ourselves to every man's conscience in the sight of God. And even if our gospel is veiled, it is veiled to those who are perishing, in whose case the god of this world has blinded

the minds of the unbelieving so that they might not see the light of the gospel of the glory of Christ, who is the image of God" (2 Corinthians 4:1-4).

Don't lose heart, Paul says, for it's discouraging to see little obvious response to the Gospel. If our Gospel is veiled, Paul reminds us, it's veiled in the hearts and minds of unbelievers. Satan blinds the unbelieving to the light of the knowledge of the glory of God – including in the first instance, the glory of God seen in the giving of the Law through Moses in Old Testament times (see 2 Corinthians 3:7; Exodus 20). This ought, in God's plan, to have led to the fullest glory of God becoming visible in Christ.

But, in the first instance, with the glory of the Law, we're talking about the glory of the judge: God in all his righteousness, his holy justice. Many today have been brought up to think we're here as a result of time and chance. We're all simply recycled star stuff from a cosmic accident. How can we tell if we crawled out of a warm pond and ascended ever upwards by sheer fluke from microbe to man? We can at least begin to answer that by noticing that we not only make factual statements such as 'you speak the truth', but we also often use sentences that carry a sense of obligation or expectation, such as 'you **should** speak the truth.'

This brings us into the territory of recognizing something as our moral duty. Philosophers debate whether an awareness of moral obligations is in fact really an awareness of God's commands or divine laws. If it is so, then the ordinary person who is aware of moral obligations does have a kind of awareness of God. This agrees with the Bible when it tells us that God has put eternity in our hearts (Ecclesiastes 3:11). An argument for God's existence from such obligations can easily be drawn up as follows:

1. There are objective moral obligations.
2. God provides the best explanation of the existence of moral obligations.
3. Then, or at very least probably, God exists.

Truth such as 'It is wrong intentionally to kill innocent humans' holds universally and is necessarily true. According to British philosopher Richard Swinburne (2004, 218), there's no 'great probability that moral awareness will occur in a Godless universe.' The fact that we humans are even aware of moral facts is surprising and calls for an explanation. Moral beliefs are not required in order to produce survival advantage, but if God exists he has 'significant reason to bring about conscious beings with moral awareness,' since his intended purpose for humans includes making it possible for them to choose good over evil, while developing a relationship with God.

On the other hand, atheists have to deny the very existence of evil in our world. Their self-appointed spokesman says: 'In a universe of electrons and selfish genes, blind physical forces and genetic replication, some people are going to get hurt, other people are going to get lucky, and you won't find any rhyme or reason in it, nor any justice. The universe that we observe has precisely the properties we should expect if there is, at bottom, no design, no purpose, no evil, no good, nothing but pitiless indifference' (Dawkins, R., *River out of Eden: a Darwinian view of life* (Basic Books: 1995), p. 133). You simply have to remember an atrocity such as '9/11' to realize that this idea is quite unrealistic.

The religious scholar, Aquinas, argued that among human beings there are to be found those who possess such qualities as 'good, true, and noble' – but that there are gradations. Some noble people are nobler than others who are noble. When we 'grade' things in this way we are, at least implicitly, comparing them to some absolute standard, and this gradation is only possible if there is some being which has this quality to a 'maximum' extent: this being which provides the standard is also the cause or explanation of the existence of these qualities, and must be God. In Romans 3:23, Paul says: "All have sinned, and fall short of the glory of God." By the glory of God, he was referring to God's standard for us humans, made in his image. He calls us to repent, and turn to the light of the knowledge of the glory of God seen in him as the Law-giver.

7

... IN THE GLORY OF THE SAVIOUR

"The light of the knowledge of the glory of God in the face of Christ" (2 Corinthians 4:6).

In our survey of Second Corinthians chapters 3 & 4, we've referred to the light of the knowledge of the glory of God in the act of creation and in the giving of the Law with its Ten Commandments. These showed, respectively, the glory of God as our Maker and the glory of God as our Judge.

But these were referred to by the Apostle Paul merely as stepping-stones in the reasoned argument he develops in these two chapters of our Bible – chapters that are themed on glory, the glory of God. At the point where Paul describes God shining light into darkened human hearts, he made first that backward reference to the Genesis account of the creation with its famous recording of the first spoken words of God: "Let there be light." And then he comes to describe Moses receiving the two stones tablets with the first directly written words of God, namely the Ten Commandments. The point Paul particularly makes here is about the skin of Moses' face shining at that time – the result of his exposure to

God's presence on the mountain top. The Apostle Paul has reminded us that was a glory that faded over time, but the actual fading of the glory was masked by the fact that Moses wore a veil on his face so that the people couldn't see the glory as it faded away.

The reason why Paul has reviewed these historical elements is to show the excellency of the Christian message. With the coming of Jesus Christ, God has revealed his glory more fully, much more fully than ever before, in fact to the greatest degree possible. We'll let Paul take up his argument, and allow him to be the one to complete it - but not before one more clarifying comment, if I may? We're going to find Paul acknowledging that there's opposition to the Christian message of revelation from God. It's something that can bring discouragement to every Christian who witnesses to the truth of God in Christ – at least whenever that witness is rejected. Contrasting with the light, there's darkness; contrasting with the rule of God, there's rebellion. There are none so blind as those who refuse to see. At the same time, the sceptic says, 'We'd believe if there was clear evidence.' 'Why,' they ask, 'is God so well hidden if he's really there?' The following words by the Apostle Paul explain that apparent hiddenness as a veil – one that's lying over their minds. Over to Paul now ...

> "Therefore, since we have this ministry, as we received mercy, we do not lose heart, but we have renounced the things hidden because of shame, not walking in craftiness or adulterating the word of God, but by the manifestation of truth commending ourselves to every man's conscience in the sight of God. And even if our gospel is veiled, it is veiled to those who are perishing, in whose case the god of this world has blinded the minds of the unbelieving so that they might not see the light of the gospel of the glory of Christ, who is the image of God.

> For we do not preach ourselves but Christ Jesus as Lord, and ourselves as your bond-servants for Jesus' sake. For God, who said, "Light shall shine out of darkness," is the One who has shone in our hearts to give the Light of the knowledge of the glory of God in the face of Christ. But we have this treasure in earthen vessels, so that the surpassing greatness of the power will be of God and not from ourselves..." (2 Corinthians 4:1-7).

The evidence of God's existence, and his great goodness to us in Christ, is not apparent to all, for Paul says: "our Gospel is veiled." The Bible acknowledges the existence of an adversarial power. Satan blinds the unbelieving to the otherwise obvious reality of creation. Satan also blinds the unbelieving to the telling witness of transcendent morality – by which, for example, there's a universal and innate understanding that it's wrong to murder innocent children under any circumstances. But beyond those two blind spots, Satan blinds the minds of unbelievers to the gift of God's son, known in history as Jesus Christ. He is the Light and he came to fulfil the Law. The Apostle John picks up on both those points very early in the Gospel that bears his name:

> "There was the true Light which, coming into the world, enlightens every man. He was in the world, and the world was made through Him, and the world did not know Him. He came to His own, and those who were His own did not receive Him. But as many as received Him, to them He gave the right to become children of God, even to those who believe in His name, who were born, not of blood nor of the will of the flesh nor of the will of man, but of God. And the Word became flesh, and dwelt among us, and we saw His glory, glory as of the only begotten from the Father, full of grace and truth ... For the Law was given through Moses; grace and truth were realized

through Jesus Christ. No one has seen God at any time; the only begotten God who is in the bosom of the Father, He has explained Him" (John 1:9-14, 17-18).

Once, Malcolm Muggeridge was blinded to the glory of God in Christ, as the Word who became flesh, but he faced up to the bankruptcy of that way of thinking, and later in life embraced Christianity, then wrote:

"In one lifetime I have seen my own fellow countrymen ruling over a quarter of the world ... I've heard a crazed, cracked Austrian proclaim to the world the establishment of a German Reich that would last a thousand years; an Italian clown announce that he would restart the calendar to begin with his own assumption of power. I've heard a murderous Georgian brigand in the Kremlin acclaimed by the intellectual elite of the world as a wiser than Solomon ... All in one little lifetime. All gone with the wind. ... Hitler and Mussolini dead, remembered only in infamy. Stalin a forbidden name in the regime he helped found and dominate for some three decades... All in one lifetime, all gone. Gone with the wind. Behind the debris of these self-styled, sullen supermen and imperial diplomatists, there stands the gigantic figure of one person, because of whom, by whom, in whom, and through whom alone mankind might still have hope. The person of Jesus Christ."

So, in summary, he's saying: Over the wreck of time, standing tall above the debris of history, is the person of Christ – a life so powerful it reset the clocks some 2,000 years ago – and in him alone forgiveness can be found.

Picking up the Apostle Paul's language here, Christian apologist, Ravi Zacharias says it well: "The greatest pursuit of the Hebrews was light. Everything was idealized by light: "The Lord is my light and my salvation..." "The people that sat in darkness have seen a great light..." For the Hebrews the ideal was light. For the Romans the ideal was glory. The glory of the Roman empire, the glory of Caesars, the city to which all roads led, the city that wasn't built in a day. Rome symbolized glory. The Hebrews symbolized light as their ideal. The Greeks pursued knowledge. The ideal of the academy, the ideal of the sophists, the ideal of wisdom, and the ideal of knowledge. Let me retrace it: The Hebrews pursued light as an ideal, the Greeks pursued knowledge as the ideal, and the Romans pursued glory. Here is the apostle Paul, a Hebrew by birth, a citizen of Rome in a Greek city. He says in 2 Corinthians 4: "God, who caused the light to shine out of darkness, has caused His light to shine in our hearts, to give to us the light of the knowledge of the glory of God in the face of Christ Jesus our Lord." (Ravi Zacharias in "Who Are You God?")

The universe around us is the work of God's hands. The starry heavens above and the moral law within, as Kant expressed it. Both testify to the glory of God. But in Christ, God has a human face. The glory of God's revelation of himself to us shines in its fullest glory not on the face of the waters (creation); not in the face of Moses (Law), but in the face of Christ, the very pinnacle of light and knowledge and glory.

8

... IN THE GLORY OF THE SPIRIT'S WORKING IN BELIEVERS

We now come to the conclusion of our studies in Second Corinthians chapters 3 and 4. We've previously been tracking the Apostle Paul's references to the glory of God with backward glimpses to the act of creation, to the giving of the Law and supremely to the life of Jesus Christ. It was in that latter connection that the full expression was applied: namely, the light of the knowledge of the glory of God. But it appeals to me that there's a fourth place where God's glory may be seen – and that's currently in the lives of followers of Jesus Christ, and comes about as the Holy Spirit works in believers to transform them to be more and more like Christ. Obviously, Christians behaving badly are not a good advert and certainly don't promote God's glory, but that's an abnormality – and not the way it should be – which is what Paul majored on in the last section of 2 Corinthians 3. He says, Christians ...

> "... are not like Moses, who used to put a veil over his face so that the sons of Israel would not look intently at the end of what was fading away. But their minds [that's the minds of the

Israelites] were hardened; for until this very day at the reading of the old covenant the same veil remains unlifted, because it is removed in Christ. But to this day whenever Moses is read, a veil lies over their heart; but whenever a person turns to the Lord, the veil is taken away. Now the Lord is the Spirit, and where the Spirit of the Lord is, there is liberty. But we all, with unveiled face, beholding as in a mirror the glory of the Lord, are being transformed into the same image from glory to glory, just as from the Lord, the Spirit" (2 Corinthians 3:13-18).

The beginning and end of that section that we've just read are closely connected to one another. Paul begins by saying we are "not like Moses, who used to put a veil over his face …" and then Paul ends by saying "but we all, with unveiled face …" So that's Moses with a veiled face and us without one. Let's unpack that. Moses put a veil over his face so that the Israelites wouldn't see the fading afterglow of his face once he'd come away from God's presence. But we, as Christians, are not to obscure in any way the increasing brightness of our lives' testimony. In Moses' case, the reflected glory of God in his face was a decreasing or diminishing radiance; in our case, daily times in God's presence when reading our Bibles and praying to God, are to produce in us an intensifying likeness to Christ. This is something glorious, and it's all the work of the Spirit of God who resides inside every true believer on the Lord Jesus Christ.

A witnessing Christian is ideally one who has spent time in God's presence – unveiled as Moses was in his time – but the Christian also remains unveiled before others when communicating. In other words, both first beholding God and then reflecting (or mirroring) to others in an unveiled way. Sadly, as we've been tracing in previous studies, there's still a veil which is now transferred to unbelieving hearts. There, Satan blinds the unbelieving to the testimony of God's love in us. This puts a clear responsibility on us to allow our lives to radiate God's love. It's been said, hasn't it, that each of us should preach the Gospel, and if necessary use words. That, however, doesn't tell the whole story, as God's Good News is for declaring to others. Each night on television screens the daily news is announced to us. That's what you do with news: it's for announcing. And so we also should present the Good News of the Christian faith – as well as letting our lives display God's glory. But the lives of Christians are the only Gospel some people will ever read ... as they see the ever-brightening after-glow coming from transformed lives. We spoke a moment ago about allowing our lives to radiate God's love. The Apostle John makes the point well about how the story of God's love is completed in us (1 John 4). Let's allow him to present to us all that he has to tell us about the love of God. It's found in First John chapter 4, from verse 7:

> "Beloved, let us love one another, for love is from God; and everyone who loves is born of God and knows God. The one who does not love does not know God, for God is love. By this the love of God was manifested in us, that God has sent His only begotten Son into the world so that we might live through Him. In this is love, not that we loved God, but that He loved us and sent His Son to be the propitiation for our sins. Beloved, if God so loved us, we also ought to love one another. No one has seen God at any time; if we love one another, God abides in us, and His love is perfected in us. By this we know that we abide in Him and He in us, because He has given us of His Spirit. We have seen and testify that the Father has sent the Son to be the Savior of the world. Whoever confesses that Jesus is the Son of God, God abides in him, and he in God.
>
> We have come to know and have believed the love which God

has for us. God is love, and the one who abides in love abides in God, and God abides in him. By this, love is perfected with us, so that we may have confidence in the day of judgment; because as He is, so also are we in this world. There is no fear in love; but perfect love casts out fear, because fear involves punishment, and the one who fears is not perfected in love" (1 John 4:7-18).

The Apostle John begins by telling us that God is love. It's what God is by nature. But then John adds that no one has seen God at any time. Love is therefore the nature of the invisible God. To reveal his love to us – to show to us what we otherwise couldn't see, God sent his son, Jesus, into this world. In his love for us, he sent his son as the man Jesus. Jesus came as God robed in mortal flesh, as one hymnwriter has put it. And the point that leads on to is the fact that God sent his son to die for the sins of all who believe on him. In summary, until this point, what John has told us is that God, by his very nature, is love. And more than that, he has displayed historically the love that he is by sending his son, Jesus Christ to die for sinners. But Christ's death and resurrection in history was almost 2,000 years ago, so is there not a present-day witness to God's love? Is it possible that God has left himself without witnesses to his love for humanity? No, God's witnesses are Christians. When John writes that God's love is perfected in us, the sense of that is God's love is - or should be -made complete in us.

I find it quite wonderful that we who believe on Christ, living believers today, can be spoken of here as completing God's purpose of declaring who he is: that he is love by his very nature. John has made three points clear about the love of God. He says God is love, and that he showed that in sending Christ, and now he completes the picture through present-day Christians. That's a billing we've got to live up to!

The Apostle John writes of love as being the characteristic feature of Christian believers: we love because we've been forgiven. On the other hand, non-believers are characterised by fear: consciously or unconsciously, there is the fear of punishment in the judgement to come. Deep in the human consciousness, the unbeliever knows that he or she is guilty before a holy God. That's why John could say in verse 18: "perfect love casts out fear, because fear involves punishment, and the one who fears is not perfected in love." Some take those words as of general application, but they're to be found in this context we've been considering. When a person repents of being a sinner and receives Christ by faith for salvation from the judgement to come, it's then that perfect love casts out fear. They then bask in God's forgiving love, free from all fear of punishment to come. Now, love, not fear, characterizes them. Returning now to where we were in 2 Corinthians, where we remember Paul having said:

> "For God, who said, "Light shall shine out of darkness," is the One who has shone in our hearts to give the Light of the knowledge of the glory of God in the face of Christ. But we have this treasure in earthen vessels, so that the surpassing greatness of the power will be of God and not from ourselves; we are afflicted in every way, but not crushed; perplexed, but not despairing; persecuted, but not forsaken; struck down, but not destroyed; always carrying about in the body the dying of Jesus, so that the life of Jesus also may be manifested in our body. For we who live are constantly being delivered over to death for Jesus' sake, so that the life of Jesus also may be manifested in our mortal flesh" (2 Corinthians 4:6-11).

Paul is referring to the 'earthen vessels' of our human bodies. He's mentioning they contain the treasure of knowing and sharing the love of

God with others. Our very weakness and inadequacy underlines that it's all done by God's own power through us. In fact, our trials, - and perhaps for some, persecutions as with Paul himself - only serve to make even more authentic our testimony to a resurrected Saviour. By the Spirit of God's transforming work of grace in us, and through the loving response he enables within us, God will be glorified.

III

HAVING A LEG TO STAND ON IN THE GOD DEBATE

Perhaps one of the most intimidating and hardest aspects of sharing the gospel is engaging in debate about the existence of God, perhaps with a hardline atheist who seems to have a range of arguments. However, this section outlines 4 key areas that we can focus on to support the case for God's existence – creation, conscience, communication (of God's Word) and the person of Christ.

9

CREATION

It's a slang English expression – the saying 'he doesn't have a leg to stand on' – but perhaps most will have heard of it. In any case, if you haven't, it means a person can't even begin to defend his or her point of view. What you may not be aware of is the fact that more or less that very same expression is found in the New Testament of the Bible – twice in fact, and both within the space of a few verses found towards the end of Romans chapter one and beginning of chapter two.

'Apologetics' is the name given to defending Christianity. Which is what we're called on to do in 1 Peter 3:15 – that is, to make a defence of the Christian hope within us. Sometimes, it seems as if we're on the back foot when doing this. The Media, often with inaccurate conclusions drawn from an all too simplistic misunderstanding of science, dismisses what it scornfully sees as our indefensible position. At times an atheistic scientist promotes a one-sided account of his or her specialist subject and so becomes the Media's favourite poster child. Even an expert scientist can be a very amateur philosopher, and straying into that territory he or she can make an impressive but flawed attack on Christianity.

The Bible calls upon Christians to make a defence of their position. But it goes even further than that. It goes on the offensive. And it does that in the section of the Bible letter which the apostle Paul wrote to the Christians who were then at Rome. This is the section we've already referred to, which is around the end of Romans chapter one. Twice, very boldly, the Bible says there (Romans 1:20; 2:1) that it's those who refuse to acknowledge God who are quite literally in an indefensible position! They are said to be 'without excuse,' meaning they have no defence. Of course, they'd be the last people to think that! This is very far from their perception of reality while they continue to "suppress the truth" (1:18), having "exchanged the truth of God for a lie" (1:25) – for "even though they knew God" (1:21), they no longer "see fit to acknowledge God" (1:28). In place of the popular assumption that it's Christianity which doesn't have a leg to stand on, the Bible presents the opposite view that it's actually atheism which has no leg to stand on. (Today's atheism as well as polytheism (and deviant monotheism) all fit the context of Romans chapter 1.)

But, as we all know, it's one thing to make a claim, it's quite another matter to support it convincingly with compelling arguments. But Paul goes on to do exactly that. In fact, he gives four main supports. All are contained in the first three chapters of the letter which was first written to the Romans and which is preserved as the sixth book of the New Testament. And in this series of studies, I'd like to look at each one of them in turn. We begin with the first, which is found in Romans chapter one, and concerns the evidence from creation all around us. Its testimony points to the existence of the one true God whom the Bible reveals. Here's how the apostle Paul makes that point first in Romans 1 verse 20: "For [God's] invisible attributes, namely, his eternal power and divine nature, have been clearly perceived, ever since the creation of the world, in the things that have been made. So they [that is, those who deny the true Creator God] are without excuse."

Simply put, what Paul is saying is this: creation is evidence of a Creator, as design is evidence for a Designer. In particular life is evidence for a life-giver in the shape of the living God. The extremely delicate complexity of the arrangements necessary for life on this planet are far less well explained by the assumption or belief that life is purely the result of an accidental combination of chance events. Then, again, in the words of Stephen Hawking "The laws of science, as we know them at present, contain many fundamental numbers – [these numbers are associated with gravity, magnetism, nuclear energy, how carbon-based life works and indeed how the universe is expanding, … Hawking continues] - the remarkable fact is that the values of these numbers seem to have been very finely adjusted to make possible the development of life." Scientists say that if any one of these numbers was different by as little as one part in a thousand, life as we know it would not seem possible.

And this is such a remarkable fact that Antony Flew, an academic philosopher who promoted atheism for most of his adult life, stated that the fine-tuned universe arguments convinced him to the point where he said, "I am very much impressed [with] the case for Christianity" (*There Is A God*, by A. Flew). It was as if he finally accepted that he was 'without excuse' in refusing to believe in God. His last book is called *'There is a God: how the world's most notorious atheist changed his mind.'*

Some strident atheist voices today are quite mistaken as to the true nature of faith, and seem to think it's only some kind of poor substitute for evidence. They keep demanding that we should go by empirical results – meaning opinions based on experience and observation rather than vague theory. Well then, science at its most empirical says; life comes from life; life doesn't come from non-life. The ancient Greeks had believed that small animals such as worms, mice, and maggots sprang to life automatically from the non-living matter around (such as rotting flour, a sweaty shirt, or decaying meat). This belief that living matter arose from non-living material is called spontaneous generation. The idea of maggots coming spontaneously to life out of decaying meat was successfully challenged in 1668 by Italian biologist Francesco Redi. When he covered the meat with gauze to prevent flies from laying their eggs on it, no maggots appeared in the meat. (The maggots are actually the larvae which hatch from flies' eggs.)

150 years ago, Frenchman Louis Pasteur confirmed this result, proving once and for all that spontaneous generation doesn't happen. In which case, there's no empirical evidence for life arising without the necessity for the existence of God. There's no such thing as a simple cell. The so-called simplest bacterial cell is still a veritable factory of a hundred thousand million atoms - much more complex than anything which we humans have ever made. The gulf between this and anything non-living is as vast and absolute as anyone could care to imagine. Antony Flew, the converted atheist whose comments about the fine-tuned universe we quoted earlier, also concluded from the microscopic world of the cell that the almost unbelievable complexity of the arrangements which are needed to produce (life) shows that intelligence must have been involved.

But you may vaguely remember a headline some time ago claiming life had been artificially created in the laboratory (the work of Craig Venter). Headlines are, however, often misleading. Let's try to explain what really happened. Just as computers use a computer code made up of programmed instructions; the cells in our body use the genetic code. In other words, cells process information (in order to make proteins and other cell bits) in a similar way to computers. The living cell is like an incredibly powerful computer. What was done recently in that publicised lab experiment, was the equivalent of making a careful copy of one version of Microsoft Windows, and turning to another computer which had previously been using a different version of Microsoft Windows and loading instead this new copy version onto it, so that when we next switch it on, that computer can now do some things it couldn't do before. But this process doesn't involve developing a totally new brand of software, nor does it involve building computer hardware that didn't exist previously. It used a software design and a computer which already existed - which means the headline about life having been created in the laboratory was very misleading.

We said cells are like computers, and most of the workings of the cell are best described, not in terms of material stuff – which we might call the hardware - but in terms of information or software. So, trying to make life by just mixing chemicals in a test tube – as in earlier laboratory experiments (e.g. Stanley Miller's) - is like soldering switches and wires in an attempt to produce Microsoft Windows. That's confusing hardware with software. Which leaves scientists (e.g. Paul Davies) to this very day still puzzling over how life could have arisen from non-living chemicals. The key question is how did the hardware of non-living molecules ever manage to write its own software?

Understanding the chemistry as we do still doesn't help us explain the origin of information. It's clear that the physical layout of letters on a printed page is independent of the chemical make-up of that printed page, and it's also true that the physical order of the chemical DNA letters is independent of their chemistry. But it's precisely the arrangement of letters – either on a page or in our cells – that gives meaning and holds the vital information. And so it follows that chemistry experiments can never explain life's origin. Only the existence of God can explain the origin of information, and so atheism is indefensible.

10

CONSCIENCE

Each summer I'm involved, with many others, in running Bible camps for youngsters. The aim is to train young people to think through for themselves what the Bible teaches. Camps like this have been taking place for many decades around the world. They're still effective. They're even seen to be effective. That must be the case, because they're being copied by those who have an alternative agenda. Rival camps have in recent years been launched in the United Kingdom (e.g. CampQuest UK) – camps which are aimed at promoting a humanist or atheist philosophy. Promotional material for these camps stress they aim to encourage critical thinking and a scientific approach - all geared to helping youth reach their own conclusions.

Well, any Christian camp I've ever been involved in has also aimed to encourage critical thinking skills and personal decision-making. So what's the difference? Simply a different framework of beliefs. No evidence – certainly none about past events – speaks for itself. It has to be evaluated using critical thinking. But that thinking itself operates based on a set of background beliefs or assumptions - whether atheistic or Christian. To imply otherwise is to admit we're self-deceived. For the reality that all human reasoning takes place within a framework of beliefs has readily been acknowledged by some great men of science (e.g. Michael Polanyi FRS, 1891-1976). The whole point then becomes: which belief system is the best to reason from while explaining the evidence? At the beginning of the letter to the Romans, the apostle Paul sets out how the Christian belief system can be easily defended.

This, it has to be said, was not his primary goal, but in the space of the first three chapters of Romans, the apostle Paul uses no less than four arguments which can serve the purpose of defending the Christian faith at the most basic point of arguing for the existence of God. And the provocative claim of the Bible found twice in Romans chapters one and two is that it's really the humanists and atheists (as well as polytheists and deviant monotheists) who have no defence – who don't have a leg to stand on – who are simply 'without excuse.'

In this series of four studies we're looking at each one of Paul's four arguments in turn. We come now to the second, which is found in Romans chapter two, and concerns the testimony of our conscience. Here's what Paul has to say:

> "For when Gentiles who do not have the Law do instinctively the things of the Law, these, not having the Law, are a law to themselves, in that they show the work of the Law written in their hearts, their conscience bearing witness and their thoughts alternately accusing or else defending them, on the day when, according to my gospel, God will judge the secrets of men through Christ Jesus" (Romans 2:14-16).

Many everyday expressions in the western world have come from the Bible in its King James Version form. And what we've just read contains an example – when we read the words: 'a law to themselves.' Interestingly, when we hear people being accused of being a law to themselves, it seems to be generally implying that they're rebellious and out of control. But that's not how the Bible uses it here. In fact, it's the very opposite! Paul was saying that it was to the Jews that the Law with its Ten Commandments was given. These commands weren't formally given to non-Jews or Gentiles. But even so, when Gentiles end up doing, by instinct, the very things which the Law commands then they're demonstrating that the same Law has in fact been written on all our hearts. It's actually correct behaviour that's evidence of a hidden law – written, not on external stone tables – but actually inside us on the tables of human hearts. And will you notice please that Paul describes it as 'the Law': it's God's Law. This Law, written on human hearts, is the basis for our conscience. And it's this that shows that we're moral beings.

But how is this a second evidence for God's existence? Paul's already used the wonder of creation as his first evidence for God's existence back in chapter one of Romans (v.20); now in chapter two (v.15) he proceeds to a second form of evidence. Because it's here, as we've seen, that he draws our attention to 'the moral Law within' (Kant). Yes, those last 3 words were quoted from Immanuel Kant, the 18th century German philosopher, who said "Two things fill the mind with ever new and increasing wonder and awe: the starry heavens above me and the moral law within me." These two things mentioned by Immanuel Kant capture, respectively, the two points we're drawing out from the apostle Paul's first two chapters written to Christians at Rome.

We were asking how is this 'moral law within' a second evidence for God's existence? Well, from the atheistic point of view, apart from their social consequences, there's really nothing basically wrong with many socially unacceptable things – things like when a man rapes a woman. Because without God there isn't any absolute standard of right and wrong which imposes itself on our conscience. Without God, morality becomes nothing more than a matter of personal taste or social conditioning. This is exactly the point many people have pressed on me in conversations about faith when they try to tell me that our attitude to something like rape basically only comes down to what our parents and society have taught us. You've got to then ask them where their parents got their values from ... and where their grandparents got theirs from ... and so on all the way back to the first ever humans. And at that point it's a problem. For blind forces of nature can't explain the origin of any absolute morality.

The late J.L. Mackie of Oxford University, one of the most influential atheists of our time, admitted, "If ... there ... are objective values, they make the existence of a god more probable than it would have been without them ... [there is, he said] ... a defensible argument from morality to the existence of a god. ..." Notice his words: 'a defensible argument.' On the other hand, Paul, in Romans, has just said atheists have no defence for their claim that there is no God (Romans 1:20; 2:1), while proceeding to give at least four defences of Christianity in terms of assuring his readers of God's existence. Paul has locked horns with the atheists, and we're faced with a clear-cut choice, and it's one we can easily put to the test. Here it is. On the one hand, the Word of God says objective moral values really do exist, and deep down we all know it; on the other hand, atheism says objective, absolute moral values don't exist – while admitting that if they did exist, that would give the game away. Richard Dawkins agrees that rape is wrong but concedes that in arriving at that view, his value judgement is every bit as arbitrary as the fact we've evolved 5 fingers rather than 6. We quote professors Mackie and Dawkins only so as to give assurance that atheists as well as Christians agree on this as a fair test. It's fair and accurate to judge the question of God's existence based on judging the question of the existence or otherwise of objective, absolute moral values.

Well then, suppose you take a group of people and ask each of them 'Do you like vegetables?' Some will say 'I like vegetables,' others will say 'I don't like vegetables.' And that's fine. It's a subjective thing, a matter of personal taste. But what if instead of asking the question 'Do you like vegetables?' we were to ask 'Is it okay to torture children for fun?' You'll surely agree that we've crossed a boundary line. You wouldn't expect the same group of reasonable people whose personal tastes on vegetables varied, to show the same spread of opinion on this question, would you? But why not? Because – I submit – this is no longer a subjective matter of personal taste, we've moved on to an altogether different matter: one that's an objective matter of right and wrong.

One famous writer (C. S. Lewis) illustrates the difference by making this comparison, he said: 'The reason my idea of New York city can be truer than yours is because New York is a real place existing apart from what either of us thinks.' On the other hand, if we were trying to compare ideas about some imaginary city, then neither idea could be truer than the other because there's no basis for any comparison. Our first example about vegetables was like that, but returning to our second example of torturing children, the reason why we'd agree that one reaction is truer than the other is because a real standard of absolute morality exists apart from whatever happen to be our own personal tastes and preferences. Torturing children for fun is not a morally neutral act – it's an outrageous moral abomination. It wouldn't matter in which culture we performed the experiment. We've identified a consensus on morality which transcends culture.

Actions like rape, torture, child abuse, and so forth, aren't just socially unacceptable behaviour. They're moral abominations: things which are absolutely wrong. Similarly, love, equality, generosity, and self-sacrifice are really good. And the point is this: if objective values cannot exist without God, but we find that they do exist, then it logically follows that God also exists.

11

COMMUNICATION

Atheism is indefensible. How often have you heard anyone say that? Probably not very often, or not at all nowadays! But the Bible goes on the offensive in the early chapters of the apostle Paul's letter to the Romans. Twice, very boldly, the Bible says around the end of Romans chapter one that it's those who refuse to acknowledge God who are quite literally in an indefensible position! They are said to be 'without excuse,' meaning they have no defence. Of course, they'd be the last people to think that! This is very far from their perception of reality as they "suppress the truth" (1:18), having "exchanged the truth of God for a lie" (1:25) – for "even though they knew God" (1:21), they no longer "see fit to acknowledge God" (1:28).

This exposure of such a deep-seated agenda shows that even when we're equipped with a good defence, many debates will still not be winnable. Recent outreach experience again demonstrated this. We were out on the streets of a busy shopping centre engaging passers-by in conversation about Christianity. Aware of how sceptical the mood is in western Europe in the 21st century, we were challenging the public to demonstrate any meaning in an alternative point of view. Not a few conceded that their outlook was bleak, but they claimed to genuinely feel that there was nothing beyond. The apostle Paul was no stranger to sceptics, even in the first century.

The kind of reasoning, explaining and giving of evidence (Acts 17:2,3) which he engaged in was also balanced with discernment of the predisposition of unpersuaded sceptics. But this still resulted at the end of the day in some sneering, others requesting a second hearing, while yet others ended up believing (vv.32-34). Jesus, in his testimony before Pilate, spoke of those who were "on the side of truth" (John 18:37 NLT). They were the ones to hear his voice. Sometimes our defence will be more about honouring God than winning arguments, whenever we encounter those whom God himself has given over to a reprobate or "depraved mind" (1:28).

But by the time Paul reaches Romans chapter 3, he's not yet done with his audience. He's already presented two important strands of evidence. He's talked about 'the starry heavens above and the moral law within.' Both point to the God who's there. But now, at the beginning of Romans chapter 3, the apostle Paul introduces a third supporting strand of evidence. Evidence which supports the contention that God exists. Paul asks: "Then what advantage has the Jew? Or what is the benefit of circumcision? Great in every respect. First of all, that they were entrusted with the oracles of God" (Romans 3:1-2). By 'oracles,' Paul is speaking about God's revelation, especially in its written form as had been entrusted to the Jewish people in terms of the writings of Moses and the other prophets as well as the writers of psalms like King David. Including now the New Testament, to which Paul himself contributed 13 letters, the completed Bible was written over a period of some 1600 years and penned by some 40 different individuals over that time.

What's more, the Bible contains many predictions. In fact, it's been estimated that at the time of writing some 25% of the Bible was prophecy, in other words claims about the future. Now, anyone can make predictions, but having those prophecies fulfilled is something else. What's the chance, for example, of predicting in which city some future world leader is going to be born? Or the exact way in which he's going to meet his death? But this is what the Bible did – hundreds of years in advance of the events. The late Professor Emeritus of Mathematics and Astronomy at Pasadena City College, Peter Stoner actually calculated the chance or probability of one man fulfilling the major prophecies made in advance in the Bible about the Messiah, Jesus. The estimates were worked out by twelve different classes which amounted to some 600 university students. Professor Stoner also encouraged other sceptics or scientists to make their own estimates to see if his conclusions were more than fair. Finally, he submitted his figures for review to a committee of the American Scientific Affiliation (Peter Stoner, Science Speaks, Chicago: Moody Press, 1969, 4).

For example, concerning Micah 5:2 which says that the Messiah would be born in Bethlehem, Stoner and his students determined the average population of Bethlehem from the time of the prophet Micah right through to the present; and then they divided it by the average world population over the same period. By expressing that ratio, they calculated that the chance of one particular man being born in Bethlehem was one in 300,000 (in the same sense as the chance of getting 'heads' in any one flipping of a coin is one in two).

Then they examined not one but eight different Bible prophecies about Jesus, the Messiah. The likelihood of them all being true by chance was found to be so small that we'll have to describe it by means of an illustration. If you make a mark on one out of ten tickets, and then place all the tickets in a hat, and thoroughly stir them, and then ask a blindfolded man to draw one, his chance of getting the one ticket which you've marked is one in ten. Now suppose that instead of tickets we take silver dollar coins - and not just 10 of them – but we take a big, big number of coins. Next, let's suppose we lay all these silver dollars all over the state of Texas in the US until we cover the whole of that state to a depth of two feet or, in other words, to a depth of about 60 centimetres. Now once again let's mark just one out of all these silver dollars and stir the whole lot of them thoroughly, all over the state.

By the way, you may be interested to know that Texas is almost 3 times the size (area) of the UK. Once again we're going to blindfold a man and tell him that he can travel as far as he wishes within Texas, but he must pick up just one silver dollar and hope that it's the right one. What chance would he have of getting the right one? It's 1 in 1 followed by 17 zeros - just the same chance, Professor Stoner worked out, that the prophets would've had of writing these eight prophecies and having them all come true in any one man, from their day to the present time, providing they wrote them in their own wisdom alone, assuming God had nothing to do with the Bible.

But, of course, there are many more than eight prophecies. In another calculation, Stoner used 48 prophecies and arrived at the estimate that the probability of 48 prophecies being fulfilled in one person is one chance in an exceedingly large number, a number which is a 1 followed by 157 zeros! Remember, for the sake of comparison, a one in a million chance is one chance in a number which is a 1 followed by only 6 zeros. But here we're talking about one chance in a number which is 1 followed by – not 6 – but 157 zeros. So, to all intents and purposes, 48 Bible prophecies have a zero chance of being fulfilled on the basis of blind chance!

But even that's the result of considering only 48 of the Bible predictions about the coming Messiah – all of which in fact came true in Jesus of Nazareth hundreds of years later. One Bible expert (Edersheim) reckons there were actually up to 456 different prophecies available for Professor Stoner to select from had he so wished. Obviously, the chance of all this being pure coincidence is vanishingly small. There can really only be one explanation for the Bible. One preacher, R.A. Torrey, put it this way. He said suppose stones for a temple were brought from quarries in Rutland, Vermont, Berea, Ohio, Kasota, Minnesota, Middleton and Connecticut. Each stone was first hewn into its final shape at its own quarry before being transported to the actual temple site. Among the stones was a great variety of sizes and shapes, like cubes and cylinders. But when they were all brought together, it turned out that every stone fitted perfectly into its allotted place. What would that show? It would show, Torrey said, that at the back of all these individual quarry workers was a single architectural mastermind.

Then he said, it's exactly like that with God's temple of truth: the Bible. How else could some 40 different human authors contribute to this one, vast project spanning some 1600 years from start to completion? The marvellous cohesion, the wonderful consistency of the Bible, with its focus on the central picture of Christ can only mean one thing – that behind all those individual human authors there stands one divine author, who masterminded the Bible as his communication to this world.

12

CHRIST

If there is a God, you'd certainly expect him to communicate, wouldn't you? And – as we saw previously - the evidence is that the Bible is just such a communication from the God who's there and who gave his Son, Jesus, for us. In the early chapters of his Bible letter to Christian believers at Rome 2,000 years ago, Paul presented four indisputable evidences which point beyond the shadow of a doubt to the existence of God. But, you may ask, have they become weakened over the 2,000 years which has since run its course? Not a bit of it! In fact, they seem much more impressive today than they could ever have appeared 2,000 years ago.

And they're easy to remember. You can remember them as all beginning with the letter C. There's the evidence from Creation (Romans 1:20); the evidence from human Conscience (2:14-16); and in the last chapter we thought about the evidence of Communication (3:1,2) as we considered the claim of the Bible to be the Word of God – a direct communication to us from the God who's there. To complete our list of 4 C's, we have Christ himself. And so we come to what Paul writes in Romans chapter 3:23-25: "for all have sinned and fall short of the glory of God, being justified as a gift by His grace through the redemption which is in Christ Jesus; whom God displayed publicly as a propitiation [or sin-atoning sacrifice] in His blood through faith."

One very clear case of atheists not having a leg to stand on occurs in connection with what Professor Richard Dawkins says about Jesus Christ. He says: 'It is possible to make a serious case that Jesus never existed.' This is nonsense. I'll confine my comments to two points. First of all, the historian Tacitus – no connection with the Bible - wrote in 115AD of Jesus' existence by recording how Nero in AD64 put the blame for the fire of Rome onto the hated class of Christians so-named after their founder who he states suffered the death penalty during the reign of Tiberius at the hands of the then governor Pontius Pilate. Then there's W.H. Lecky, who wrote a history of Europe in which he stated that the impact of the three public years of Jesus' ministry had a more profound impact than all the writings of moralists and philosophers have ever had.

More recently, former US president Ronald Reagan made a similar point when he said: 'meaning no disrespect to the religious convictions of others, I still can't help wondering how we can explain away what to me is the greatest miracle of all and which is recorded in history. No one denies there was such a man, that he lived and that he was put to death by crucifixion. Where ... is the miracle I spoke of? Well, consider this and let your imagination translate the story into our own time — possibly to your own home town. A young man whose father is a carpenter grows up working in his father's shop. One day he puts down his tools and walks out of his father's shop. He starts preaching on street corners and in the nearby countryside, walking from place to place, preaching all the while, even though he is not an ordained minister. He does this for three years. Then he is arrested, tried and convicted. There is no court of appeal, so he is executed at age 33 along with two common thieves. Those in charge of his execution roll dice to see who gets his clothing — the only possessions he has. His family cannot afford a burial place for him so he is interred in a borrowed tomb. End of story? No, this uneducated, propertyless young man who...left no written word has, for 2000 years, had a greater effect on the world than all the rulers, kings, emperors; all the conquerors, generals and admirals, all the scholars, scientists and philosophers who have ever lived — all of them put together. How do we explain that?...unless he really was who he said he was."

Notice Reagan, when he spoke of Jesus' historical existence as indisputable, said the opposite of what Dawkins stated. In fact, there's much more documentary evidence for the life of Jesus Christ than there is for Julius Caesar – and you don't hear many people questioning Caesar as a historical character, do you?

No fictional life could have the lasting impact which the life of Christ has had. Christianity continues as it began – with the testimony of transformed lives. One of the primary evidences for the resurrection of Jesus Christ from the dead on the third day is the radical transformation of the earliest disciples from being fearful to becoming fearless witnesses who were prepared to die for their beliefs. But there are other major evidences for Jesus' resurrection, like the fact that it's exceedingly unlikely that a whole bunch of people were prepared to die for a hoax or lie which they had deliberately invented.

Then there's the evidence of a generation of numerous eye-witnesses to the resurrected Christ; and the clearest evidence of all – which people hostile to Christianity at that time tried to actively suppress – the empty tomb itself. Its existence – empty existence – was conceded by those who had everything to gain by simply producing a body – if they could.

Yes, you can explore all the options – like Jesus only swooned and later revived; or his body was stolen; or his gullible followers were only hallucinating – but none of these fit the facts as well as the account which says Jesus actually did rise from the dead. But don't just take my word for it. Simon Greenleaf was a professor at Harvard. A professor of Law, in fact: an expert in handling the laws of evidence. He was supremely qualified to make a pronouncement on the quality of the evidence for the resurrection of Jesus Christ after making a detailed study of all of it. And he did this from an initial sceptical point of view. He set out – as others have done – to demolish the myth of Jesus rising from the dead, but his integrity forced him to change his opinion completely once he'd studied everything. He concluded that the resurrection of Jesus Christ was, in fact, the best supported event in all history.

The apostle Paul says that if Christ has not been raised from the dead then our faith is vain (1 Corinthians 15:14) – in other words he admits this one event of Jesus' resurrection is the all-important test. And the thing is it's something which can be tested – it's not something purely subjective in the mind of the believer. We can do what Simon Greenleaf did. There's this real objective test which is decisive for Christianity – and in this post-modern age that's vitally important. If you're serious about discovering the truth, you owe it to yourself to really investigate this one claim that Jesus did rise from the dead.

I also like to quote the refreshingly frank and even eloquent tribute given thoughtfully by Napoleon Bonaparte after he'd a lot of time to think during a period of exile in his life. It's recorded that he said to one of his associates that he, Napoleon, had inspired multitudes with such an enthusiastic devotion that they'd have died for him. But he said to do that it'd been necessary for him to be visibly present with the electric influence of his looks, words and voice. Napoleon went on to say that

Christ alone had succeeded in so raising the mind of man toward the unseen that it became insensible to the barrier of time and space. Across a chasm of 1800 years, Jesus Christ, he said, made a demand which is beyond all others difficult to satisfy ... [Jesus] asks for the human heart. He demands it unconditionally and forthwith his demand is granted." Wonderful! In defiance of time and space, the spirit of man with all its powers and faculties becomes an annexation to the empire of Christ. All who sincerely believe experience that supernatural love towards him. Napoleon commented that this phenomenon is unaccountable, and he said it was this that showed convincingly the divinity of Jesus Christ.

And so as we bring this series to a close, we remind ourselves we've been looking at the early chapters of Paul's Bible letter to Christian believers at Rome 2,000 years ago. There Paul presents four indisputable evidences which point beyond the shadow of a doubt to the existence of God. And they're easy to remember. You can remember them as all beginning with the letter C. There's the evidence from Creation (Romans 1:20); the evidence from human Conscience (2:14-16); the evidence of Communication (3:1,2) as we considered the claim of the Bible to be the Word of God – a direct communication to us from the God who's there; and there's the best evidence of all - completing our list of 4 C's - Christ himself.

Finally, let me tell you about a woman who was catching a flight at the airport. She was in a mad rush, hadn't had time to eat on the way there, so she stops at the newsstand to buy a pack of cookies, then sits down at the gate where there's a table between her and an older man. But soon she can't believe her eyes when the man stretches over, picks up the pack of cookies from the table and helps himself to one. She's shocked, but doesn't want to make a scene, so just takes one herself, placing the pack back on the table – surely the man won't have the nerve to repeat his action! But he did! Again he picks up the pack, looks at it thoughtfully, takes another cookie and, after a little nibble, proceeds to gobble it up. By now she's pretty well hopping mad. How dare he just help himself to her cookies! Quickly she takes another herself – now there's just the one left.

Unbelievably, the chap reaches across again and picks out the last cookie, smiles, breaks it in half, and pushes the last half towards her. She's ready now to make a scene, but the boarding call comes and the chap jumps up and with another smile he's gone. At the gate the woman opens her bag to get her boarding pass and it's then she discovers her pack of cookies still in her bag – she'd been the one helping herself, not him! The moral of that is that sometimes reality is a lot different from what we think – and we're in too much of a rush to check it out. We have our misconceived ideas about where we come from / what the purpose of life is / and where we're going afterwards, because we just feed on what society around us tells us - all the time wrongly believing it to be the truth. I urge you to take a fresh look at things! Please check out whose bag of cookies you've been eating from!

IV

USING PICTURES OF SALVATION

Once we've connected with our audience and broken up the stony ground for the seed of the Gospel, we can gently introduce them to the Bible's teaching about the cross of Christ and what it means. The Apostle Paul skillfully, under God, employed what was then everyday language, and related to very familiar places, to make the Christian message understandable. With the sharing of some important historical background information about Roman society, we can learn from his clarity of presentation.

13

SLAVERY TO SIN - THE SLAVE MARKET (REDEMPTION)

Slavery was an accepted way of life in the Roman Empire. So much so that perhaps we could call it an institution in those days. Probably at least a quarter of all people in the empire were slaves. During the reign of Claudius, when the apostle Paul was writing his Bible letters, there was something like 20 million slaves just in Italy alone. Most slaves were domestic helps. The household was made up of husband and wife, their children, and slaves, and was the most important social unit in the Roman Empire. Slaves were involved at every level of life in the household - they took care of finances; prepared the food; dressed the householder and his family; nursed the family when sick; guarded the estate and the family; read poetry; reminded the master of people's names; provided background music at dinner; served as messengers and doorkeepers; and the women were sometimes concubines.

What could be more natural, therefore, than for the Apostle Paul to relate the Christian message of salvation to this very common practice and way of life? At that time, people understood the idea of slavery only too well, and a slave would normally dream of obtaining his or her freedom. It's hardly surprising then, that in presenting the Christian message 2,000 years ago, the apostle Paul used the emotive imagery of freedom from slavery. One place where this picture of salvation is clearly used is found in Romans chapter 6:17-18 (NIV), where Paul says: "... thanks be to God that, though you used to be slaves to sin, you wholeheartedly obeyed the form of teaching to which you were entrusted. You have been set free from sin ..."

We're all used to the appealing images used by advertisers in selling their product. Rarely, if ever, does the product deliver on the glamorous image that's implied. But with the Christian message it's exactly the opposite! No single human idea or analogy can do it justice! That's why in this series we'll be looking at the 4 main pictures Paul used at the Holy Spirit's direction to communicate what it means to experience the spiritual salvation Christianity offers. The picture of human slaves to sin being set free is just one of them – but it's an important one and it's good if we have a bit more background so that we can appreciate it better.

Back in the days of the Roman Empire, people became slaves for a number of reasons. Prisoners of war became slaves. Others were kidnapped and sold into slavery – sometimes as a result of piracy. Another source of slaves was purchase from over the boundaries of the empire. Roman soldiers involved in frontier wars and rebellions had many opportunities to buy prisoners of war as slaves at auctions. But people often became slaves simply because of poverty. Someone who couldn't pay his debts could be forced into slavery until the debt was paid in service. When a person was no longer able to obtain food and shelter, that person might make a contract to become a slave. Similarly, if a baby wasn't able to be cared for, it could be made the property of a slave owner. Individuals who were part of the slave trade either collected abandoned babies for later sale themselves or bought them from others who found them. The children of slaves also became the possession of the Master. Slavery could also be brought about by conviction in law – as a punishment for a serious crime.

In summary, it's been said: 'slaves were either born or made.' If we pursue the Bible's analogy with slavery as regards our spiritual condition, then we're made to realize that we're 'sinners by nature and by practice'. We inherit a sinful nature from our parents that's traceable all the way back to the disobedience of the first man, Adam – we're all tainted by the original sin (Romans 5:12). This expresses itself as our in-born tendency to choose to go our own way. As a result, we're all sinners by practice, and sin spoils our lives: 'for all have sinned and fall short of the glory of God' (Romans 3:23), the Bible says. And, as Jesus himself said in John 8:34: "everyone who sins is a slave to sin." This is the spiritual slavery that extends to everyone on the planet.

Sin in our lives can show itself to be a harsh master, as when it leads to the destruction of our health or the wreck of our family life. The life of a Roman slave at times paralleled this. While some slaves might've had a better life than that of poor people who were free, others were confined to the private prison attached to most Roman farms. There the slaves were made to work in chains as they cultivated the fields. The prison appears to have been usually underground, lit by narrow windows. The windows were too high from the ground to be touched by the hand. Slaves who had displeased their masters were punished by imprisonment here. It was where all slaves who could not be depended upon were housed. It all reminds me of what Paul had to say in Galatians 3:22 (NIV) - "the Scripture declares that the whole world is a prisoner of sin, so that what was promised, being given through faith in Jesus Christ, might be given to those who believe."

But, in Roman society a slave could buy freedom or someone else could pay a sum of money to obtain a slave's freedom. Freedom was sometimes given as a reward for loyalty. In one case, a woman was set free because she bore four sons who became the master's slaves. Once freedom was attained, the freed person could not be reclaimed as a slave. Sometimes a slave could actually be adopted by the master and inherit equally with the natural sons.

This brings us to the good news of Christianity: that all of us who are spiritual slaves to sin can be made free through Jesus Christ. He is the one "in whom we have redemption" (Ephesians 1:7). The word 'redemption' (apolutrosis) means 'to redeem one by paying the price, to let go free on receiving the price ... liberation ... by payment of a ransom' (Thayer). The story of redemption in the New Testament of the Bible can be told in 3 of its original words. The first, 'agorazo,' (1 Corinthians 6:20; 7:23,30; 2 Peter 2:1; Revelation 5:9) means 'to buy in the slave market.' The way it's applied in the Bible makes the wonderful story of Christianity very clear – that the Lord Jesus came to this earth as man so that he might buy us in the slave market of sin – the slave market of sin representing the degrading situation into which human disobedience had brought us.

The second word for redemption (exagorazo), a word meaning 'to buy out of the slave market,' emphasizes that the Christian believer now belongs to the Lord Jesus Christ since it was he who bought us at a price for himself. Paul asks the Corinthians Christians: "Do you not know that your body is a temple of the Holy Spirit, who is in you, whom you have received from God? You are not your own; you were bought at a price. Therefore honour God with your body" (1 Corinthians 6:19-20 NIV).

SLAVERY TO SIN - THE SLAVE MARKET (REDEMPTION)

The redeemed believer on the Lord Jesus is his possession for ever, never again to be put up for sale. The idea of a price having been paid brings us to the third word for redemption (lutroo), which means 'to liberate by payment of a ransom.' All who repent and believe on Jesus Christ are set free from the guilt and penalty of their sins. This redemption, this forgiveness of sins, is 'through his blood' – for the ransom price paid for sinners was the death of Jesus, the Son of God, when he was crucified outside Jerusalem two thousand years ago in God's plan of salvation: his plan to liberate spiritually all who believe. Let's hear more about that tremendous plan from Ephesians 1:5-8 (NIV): "[God] predestined us to be adopted as his sons through Jesus Christ, in accordance with his pleasure and will—to the praise of his glorious grace, which he has freely given us in the One he loves. In him we have redemption through his blood, the forgiveness of sins, in accordance with the riches of God's grace."

Our last thought in this study on the Bible picture of salvation as being like slaves being freed concerns the fact that believers on the Lord Jesus, the one who has bought them out of the slave market of sin, now have an obligation to live for him. This is how Paul puts it in writing to his Christian friends in Rome: "You have been set free from sin and have become slaves to righteousness ... But now that you have been set free from sin and have become slaves to God, the benefit you reap leads to holiness, and the result is eternal life. For the wages of sin is death, but the gift of God is eternal life in Christ Jesus our Lord" (Romans 6:18,22-23 NIV).

14

SENTENCED TO DEATH - THE LAW COURTS (JUSTIFICATION)

In the previous study we were thinking about society in New Testament times in the then Roman world. We were thinking about how slavery, in particular, was an everyday fact of life, and how the apostle Paul, directed by the Holy Spirit, drew upon this background in one of the main pictures of salvation he used: that of being set free from sin's spiritual slavery. It's a different kind of freedom we want to explore now. Not so much ethical, but legal. We now turn our searchlight on to another favourite source of illustration for Paul. In doing so, we make our way from the slave-market to the law courts. Paul was certainly aware of his legal rights as a Roman citizen. Once, he escaped a flogging because he asserted his rights as a Roman citizen. Paul had an incisive mind, and in his own defence at times he went head-to-head with the best advocates of the day (e.g. in Acts 24)!

Perhaps, the Roman legal system was the greatest strength of the Roman Empire, after its armies, that is. The rights of citizens were firmly upheld in the courts. Then, as today, cases in court were decided by argument between lawyers, and judgements by elected magistrates were based on earlier decisions. Roman law has had a significant influence on legal systems down to the present day – certainly in Europe. Sometimes when sharing the Christian message, Paul seems to use legal language and forensic terms, his reasoning no doubt reflecting the legal processes of the time. It's worth looking at this, because, as we say, we believe the Holy Spirit was directing Paul in his choice of the language and terms we find in the Bible.

When writing to his Christian friends at the very heart of the empire in Rome, Paul argues that all – both Gentile and Jew - have sinned. As we read through to the end of the third chapter of his letter to the Romans, it's as if the death sentence has already been passed (for such is the wages of sin) and we, the prisoners, are helplessly awaiting the inevitable on death row. There's a mounting sense of dread suspense as if the footsteps of the executioner are getting nearer and nearer to the cell on death row where the prisoner is housed. As I quote verses from these chapters, one after another, think of them as footsteps drawing nearer to a convicted prisoner:

- Romans 1:18 - "For the wrath of God is revealed from heaven against all ungodliness."
- Romans 1:28 - "God gave them over to a depraved mind, to do those things which are not proper."
- Romans 2:1 - "Therefore you have no excuse."
- Romans 2:2 - "the judgment of God rightly falls upon those who practice such things."
- Romans 2:5-6 - "But because of your stubbornness and unrepentant heart you are storing up wrath for yourself in the day of wrath and revelation of the righteous judgment of God, who WILL RENDER TO EACH PERSON ACCORDING TO HIS DEEDS."

All these verses fall like heavy footsteps, sounding louder and louder...

- Romans 3:10 - "as it is written, "THERE IS NONE RIGHTEOUS, NOT EVEN ONE..."
- Romans 3:12 - "ALL HAVE TURNED ASIDE ... THERE IS NONE WHO DOES GOOD."
- Romans 3:20 - "because by the works of the Law no flesh will be justified in His sight; for through the Law comes the knowledge of sin."
- Romans 3:23 - "for all have sinned and fall short of the glory of God ..."

These verses fall upon our ears like the unrelenting footsteps of the executioner as he draws ever nearer to our condemned cell. Condemned, convicted, and broken by the realization that all this is true, we sit and await the inevitable. It's as if we hear the hand of the executioner turn the door handle ... then suddenly at verse 24 of the third chapter, it's as if the cell door is suddenly flung open – and we read: "being justified as a gift by His grace through the redemption which is in Christ Jesus." Try to visualize it with me. It's as if light suddenly and unexpectedly pours into our cell. In a dramatic pronouncement we're declared free to go. 'Free! Made free, and not simply forgiven, but reckoned Not guilty!' Who could blame us for standing there blinking with surprise? But this is no jail-break. There's no miscarriage of justice involved in this. Not at all! Justice has been satisfied - because of the work of Christ. Paul continues by explaining that Jesus Christ, the Son of God, hung and died on the cross two thousand years ago: "for the demonstration ... of [God's] righteousness ... so that He [God] would be just and the justifier of the one who has faith in Jesus" (Romans 3:23).

It's precisely this language of justification that's taken from the legal system. It's the declaring of someone as righteous (or just). The word's a forensic one, and one that's not used in Greek literature for making righteous – but used instead for the reckoning of righteousness. It consists of the non-reckoning of sins. Romans chapter 4 is a good place to see that. In the language of one Bible version we read there in chapter 4 and verses 3 to 8:

> "ABRAHAM BELIEVED GOD, AND IT WAS CREDITED TO HIM AS RIGHTEOUSNESS." Now to the one who works, his wage is not credited as a favor, but as what is due. But to the one who does not work, but believes in Him who justifies the ungodly, his faith is credited as righteousness, just as David also speaks of the blessing on the man to whom God credits righteousness apart from works: "BLESSED ARE THOSE WHOSE LAWLESS DEEDS HAVE BEEN FORGIVEN, AND WHOSE SINS HAVE BEEN COVERED. BLESSED IS THE MAN WHOSE SIN THE LORD WILL NOT TAKE INTO ACCOUNT."

We know what it means to receive a credit (payment) on some statement of account. In a different context we may even have experienced getting credit for something we haven't done – credit we don't deserve. But isn't it amazing to think that, knowingly, God's prepared to do just that – to credit us with something we don't deserve, credit that we haven't earned! On the evidence of our faith alone – just as it was with Abraham – God is prepared to credit us with righteousness, meaning our sins will not be reckoned against us. Suddenly our guilt, our debt, the debit balance of our account with God, is transformed into credit. It's pure grace, activated on our part by personal faith, as verse 16 says: "For this reason it is by faith, in order that it may be in accordance with grace..." And returning to the story of Abraham it adds:

"Therefore IT WAS ALSO CREDITED TO HIM AS RIGHTEOUSNESS. Now not for his sake only was it written that it was credited to him, but for our sake also, to whom it will be credited, as those who believe in Him who raised Jesus our Lord from the dead, He who was delivered over because of our transgressions, and was raised because of our justification" (Romans 4:22-25 NASB).

That's Romans chapter 4, and in Romans chapter 5 (v.18) "justification" is presented as the opposite of "condemnation." This is another important picture of salvation, drawn up for us by the Spirit of God, against the background of the Roman – and subsequent - legal systems. One in which we've seen, I trust, that this Bible word 'justification' is the legal and formal acquittal from guilt by God as Judge – the declaring of a verdict of 'not guilty.' How good it is to know that we're no longer guilty before a holy God as a result of having put our faith in Jesus Christ, his son! And what a wonderful pronouncement by God the Judge – the pronouncement of the sinner as righteous, whenever he or she believes on the Lord Jesus Christ! As someone has pointed out – there's an easy way to think of the word "justified": simply sound it out as "just-as-if-I'd" never sinned!

15

UNDER GOD'S WRATH - THE TEMPLE SHRINE (PROPITIATION)

As we begin this chapter, I invite you to take a look with me at Paul's New Testament letter which he wrote to his friends in Rome. We've looked at it twice before in this series already, and I make no apology for picking it up again. For the four pictures of salvation which are the theme of this series of studies can all be found well documented in the apostle Paul's letter to the Romans. So, as I say, let's look at Romans and chapter 3 verses 24 and 25. After telling us that we all have sinned, the Holy Spirit of God through Paul continues with the good news of salvation: "being justified as a gift by His grace through the redemption which is in Christ Jesus; whom God displayed publicly as a propitiation in His blood through faith. This was to demonstrate His righteousness, because in the forbearance of God He passed over the sins previously committed."

There are three descriptions of the cross-work of Jesus there – the work Jesus Christ, the Son of God, performed when he died on a Roman cross just outside the city of Jerusalem some two thousand years ago. What took place there is first of all viewed as 'redemption.' And that, you'll remember, was the subject of an earlier study. It's a commercial term drawn from the marketplace where in the society of those days humans as well as other goods were bought and sold. We understood redemption as the idea of someone being bought out of the slave market and being given their freedom – one picture of our salvation as being from the slavery of sin.

Another way in which the cross was viewed in the two verses we read was as a 'demonstration' – a demonstration of what, you ask? A demonstration of God's justice. Previously, Paul explains, God had in his forbearance passed over sins. But the cross stands for all time to make it absolutely clear that God never at any time had the intention of ignoring them, far less condoning them. The cross was pre-planned as the demonstration of his justice. The language at this point is legal language, of course, borrowed from the law court, and we spent time on that picture of salvation in our previous study.

Now, we're going to be occupied with the third view of the cross that's found within the span of those two verses – verses 24 and 25 of Romans chapter 3. The third view of the cross is contained in the description of what happened there as being a 'propitiation.' This is an important Bible word, but one that perhaps needs even more by way of explanation than the others. If the word 'redemption' was a word that was then in use in the marketplaces; and if the word 'justification' would've been encountered in the law courts; then the word 'propitiation' would have been commonly used in the pagan temples of the time. In that setting it meant to placate or appease the angry gods which the pagans acknowledged.

At first, we might think there can be no connection between this idea of turning away anger and the biblical teaching of Christianity. After all, the living and true God who's our creator is presented to us in the pages of the Bible as being an unchanging God, certainly not fickle and petty-minded which was how the pagans viewed their gods – who were always needing to be placated. But let's take a closer look ... In these verses in Romans chapters 1, 2 and 3, Paul is describing God's solution for the human predicament, which is not only sin, but God's wrath upon sin. Perhaps today the idea of an angry God is considered less than a Christian point of view. But if our property is defaced or our loved ones come under an unprovoked attack, we would expect to feel righteous indignation against the wrong done to us. It's what we then do with that anger that can involve sinful behaviour. God's righteous anger is never uncontrolled.

We're going to have to identify exactly how this term 'propitiation' is different within a Christian understanding. The reason why it's necessary, and the one who initiates it, and even the means by which it's performed are all radically different within Christianity compared with the way in which propitiation was understood in pagan temples and the background customs of New Testament times. Remember, by propitiation we mean the turning away of God's anger.

Among the pagans the need for propitiation arose because they understood the gods to be angry simply because they were a bad-tempered bunch, always subject to mood swings. The Christian explanation of the need for turning away God's anger could not be more different. God's anger, or wrath, is his consistent antagonism against sin, his hatred of anything that's morally evil. God's holy nature cannot accommodate any wrongdoing. It remains hostile to anything which misses the mark of his glorious perfection. Next, we think of how the pagans assumed that only they could appease their gods, after all it was they who had somehow offended them. In the Christian setting, however, the Bible plainly teaches us that we cannot appease God's righteous anger – nothing we can do can make ourselves acceptable to God. But it goes on to tell us that God has done what we couldn't do. This is how the apostle John puts it:

> "In this the love of God was made manifest among us, that God sent his only Son into the world, so that we might live through him. In this is love, not that we have loved God but that he loved us and sent his Son to be the propitiation for our sins" (1 John 4:9-10).

What we couldn't do, God has done. It's what the cross was all about; at least it's one of the 3 views of it we referred to earlier from Romans chapter 3. At the cross, God's anger was turned away from us and directed at himself in the person of his son, Jesus Christ. We've got to be very clear about the fact that both the initiative and the action of this propitiation lay with God. Then there's the means by which propitiation was made. The pagans bribed their gods with various sweetmeats. This was very different from the sacrificial system we read about in the Old Testament, because even in it the people were made to understand they were giving back to God from what he'd given them in the first place. Notice how a verse in Leviticus 17 (verse 11) makes that clear: "For the life of the flesh is in the blood, and I have given it for you on the altar to make atonement for your souls, for it is the blood that makes atonement by the life." In the New Testament, it's even clearer that the work of salvation and the means by which God's wrath is turned away from us is not our own doing, but is all of God's grace.

We return to our opening text from Romans chapter 3:24-25: "being justified as a gift by His grace through the redemption which is in Christ Jesus; whom God displayed publicly as a propitiation in His blood through faith. This was to demonstrate His righteousness, because in the forbearance of God He passed over the sins previously committed." There we have it: a third biblical picture of salvation. In contrast with the previous two we've looked at – where the word concerned – be it redemption or justification – had an agreed meaning which could simply be applied to Christian teaching – we've seen that the language of the temple shrines – in particular, this word propitiation – had to be redefined or at least radically re-aligned.

In concluding, it's worth noting that Paul addressed this letter to Christian believers, calling them 'saints' (Romans 1:7) – in other words, those who had been sanctified. This terminology was also one that had a background in the pagan Greek religions. There it meant 'devoted to the gods' (Liddell and Scott). For example, if a Greek worshipper brought a gift to his god, he devoted it to that god. The gift became holy in that sense – no thought of purity in the word, but only the idea of being set apart from common use so as to be devoted to the gods. Paul can biblically describe every Christian believer as a saint in the sense that the Holy Spirit has taken each believing sinner and set him or her apart for God by placing them 'in Christ.' What's more, corresponding to that, there's to be a practical holiness – or sanctification - increasingly seen in the purity of the believer's life for the Lord Jesus. There again we have to part company with the pagan background of the word, for in the Greek thought of holiness there was no sense of morality, for the pagan religions of that time were in fact rather immoral. God's thoughts are indeed much higher than our own!

16

ALIENATED FROM GOD - THE FAMILY CIRCLE (RECONCILIATION)

To introduce our fourth and final picture of salvation – pictures we're identifying from the writings of the apostle Paul in the New Testament, we now need to introduce ourselves to what would have been in many respects a fairly typical New Testament family. So far, we've seen how Paul's pictures of salvation were drawn from the marketplace, the law courts and the pagan temple shrines. For this last picture we come much closer to home – into the circle of family life. Let's meet the family. Dad and Mum appear to be comfortably well off; well-liked, and what's more they're committed Christians. They host the gatherings of the local church in their own home, and they've a son who's active in serving the Lord. Sometime back there was real drama in the household when a domestic help ran off – with how much of the 'silverware' we're not entirely sure. The fuss soon died down, until one Sunday in church there was a dramatic announcement which contained some startling news...

Perhaps, by this stage, you may have a feeling that you already know this family from somewhere. Well, you probably do – from the pages of the

New Testament! Dad is Philemon; and Apphia is his wife. The Church of God at Colossae (in first century Turkey) meets in their home. Their son, we believe, is Archippus whom no less than the apostle Paul respects as a 'fellow soldier.' It was from this household that Onesimus ran off – and didn't stop running for a 1,000 miles until he reached Rome! That was quite a marathon – but necessary because his crime was punishable by death under Roman law.

Actually, it seems there might have been two letters to be read to the church that Sunday morning we referred to - they're the Bible letters we now know as Colossians and Philemon. Have you ever wondered why the letter to Philemon is included in the Bible? It's only 25 verses long, with no deep meaning or direct teaching – and it's generally ignored even by the Christian public. One good reason it's there is to illustrate how we can mend broken relationships. It's a prime example of how we should put Bible teaching (in Colossians) into immediate daily practice (as in Philemon).

We don't fully know why Onesimus ran away – in part it could've been to escape the gospel at home. Perhaps there's a clue (v.18) that he'd stolen 'something for his journey.' Facing a death sentence, he just kept on running. A big city like Rome was just the place to 'lose himself.' But, in fact, it was there that he 'found himself' - through meeting Paul - and through becoming a born-again Christian. Perhaps Onesimus either fell into trouble or found employment in the prison service – anyway it was in prison he met the apostle Paul – and Epaphras. He could hardly have expected to meet Epaphras who was from his hometown of Colossae 1,000 miles away, but God's providence is a wonderful thing! It's even possible that Epaphras was acquainted with some of the facts concerning Philemon and his runaway slave – who now stood before them.

We can be sure that Paul in conversation with Onesimus lost no time in telling him about his need to know Jesus Christ as saviour. Onesimus listened and by God's grace, responded. So, like Abraham, Paul had the joy of having a son in his old age – a spiritual one! And like Joseph, he'd been made fruitful in trying conditions! It was all going to work together for good: not only with Onesimus' saving faith in Christ, but with his return and reconciliation to his master! For Paul was sending him back to Colossae to be reconciled with Philemon. But he wasn't sending him back empty-handed, he and Tychicus would be carrying two letters that are now found in our Bibles. The two letters – those of Colossians and Philemon - were written and delivered at the same time (Colossians 4:7-9). 'Colossians' has the direct teaching about Christ and Christian relationships; while the letter to Philemon – which I imagine the whole church heard, too – simply contained a strikingly timed appeal to put it into immediate practice in the case of Onesimus who came with them!

Very relevant teaching for exactly that kind of real-life situation is found in the letter to the Colossians – it's this, that "there is no [distinction between] ... slave and freeman ... as those who have been chosen of God ... put on a heart of compassion, kindness, humility, gentleness and patience; bearing with one another, and forgiving each other, whoever has a complaint against anyone; just as the Lord forgave you, so also should you"(Colossians 3:11-15 NASB). And if that seemed to have a message applicable to Philemon, a little later on there was a message that was just as applicable to Onesimus, the runaway slave:

> "Slaves, in all things obey those who are your masters on earth, not with external service, as those who [merely] please men, but with sincerity of heart, fearing the Lord. Whatever you do, do your work heartily, as for the Lord rather than for men ... For he who does wrong will receive the consequences of the

wrong which he has done, and that without partiality. Masters, grant to your slaves justice and fairness, knowing that you too have a Master in heaven" (Colossians 3:18-4:1 NASB).

How often have we heard Bible teaching and been slow to put it into practice? They had an immediate opportunity brought before them in the second letter! In the more personal letter to Philemon, Paul urged Philemon to apply the teaching on reconciliation and forgiveness. What this demonstrates – quite dramatically – is the fact that reconciliation is readily associated with and frequently needed in family life - or life within a household - which in those days included domestic slaves. Reconciliation with one another is one thing – albeit an important matter – but Paul spoke of our need of salvation in terms of our need to be reconciled with God. In his second letter to Corinth he put it like this:

> "If anyone is in Christ, he is a new creature; the old things passed away; behold, new things have come. Now all these things are from God, who reconciled us to Himself through Christ and gave us the ministry of reconciliation, namely, that God was in Christ reconciling the world to Himself, not counting their trespasses against them, and He has committed to us the word of reconciliation. Therefore, we are ambassadors for Christ, as though God were making an appeal through us; we beg you on behalf of Christ, be reconciled to God" (2 Corinthians 5:17-20).

Reconciliation, then, is another of the major words that explain and illustrate the Christian message of salvation. Perhaps we're reminded of another story told by Jesus – the story not of the runaway slave, but of the runaway son. In Luke chapter 15 we read how this young man demanded his share of his father's inheritance and then left home and spent it wastefully. Soon he was deserted by the friends he had while his money lasted, and being in debt, he was reduced to feeding pigs. It was there he came to his senses and determined to return to his father and throw himself on his mercy. If only he might hope that his father would allow him to live in the lean-to behind the cowshed, he'd be prepared to earn his passage among the hired hands on his father's farm. But when he turns around and goes to meet his father and blurts out his confession: 'I have sinned'; he discovers his father's been waiting for him and he's welcomed back as a son with great rejoicing.

Sin – our natural tendency to go our own way - is the thing that spoils our lives. It separates us from God, we're estranged from him and our debt against him accumulates. When God's Spirit works in our hearts we, too, come to our senses, and whenever we throw ourselves upon God's mercy, asking for the forgiveness that's found in Jesus Christ, his son, we discover something more than we could ever have expected: we discover God as a Father who welcomes us into his own family. When we turn from our sins and turn to God – when we receive Jesus Christ by faith, we find ourselves reconciled to God - and born again as a child of God (John 1:12), and adopted as a legal heir of a glorious heavenly inheritance (Ephesians 1:5; 1 Peter 1:3,4). Isn't that wonderful?

Reconciliation is a great Bible word explaining the Christian message of salvation as the mending of our broken relationship with God. And with it, we end this little series on pictures of salvation – a series which has seen us visit the marketplace, the law courts and the temple shrines as well as the more homely family setting.

ABOUT THE AUTHOR

Born and educated in Scotland, Brian worked as a government scientist until God called him into full-time Christian ministry on behalf of the Churches of God (www.churchesofgod.info). His voice has been heard on Search For Truth radio broadcasts for over 30 years (visit www.searchfortruth.podbean.com) during which time he has been an itinerant Bible teacher throughout the UK. His evangelical and missionary work outside the UK is primarily in Belgium, The Philippines and South East Central Africa. He is married to Rosemary, with a son and daughter.

MORE BOOKS FROM BRIAN JOHNSTON

MINDFULNESS THAT JESUS ENDORSES

Mindfulness is the trendy meditation offshoot recently endorsed by everyone from National Health Service departments in the UK to Oprah Winfrey in the US. In view of its possible Buddhist origins and the danger of becoming self-absorbed, is there a such a thing as a Biblical Mindfulness that Jesus could endorse? That's the question that Brian answers as he re-introduces us to the transforming power of biblical meditation which, instead of emptying the mind, fills it with a sense of the presence and immediacy of God, and His relevance to what we're experiencing at any moment.

MINOR PROPHETS? MAJOR ISSUES!

The so-called "Minor Prophets" of the Old Testament, such as Nahum, Micah and Malachi, are often overlooked because of their brevity and also because they might seem irrelevant to Christians of today. Brian shows how inaccurate this perception is by pointing out that each prophet not only had vital things to say to the peoples of that era, but they also raise very major issues that are absolutely relevant to believers today. Such issues include: injustice, suffering, unfaithfulness, abandonment, corruption, compassion, arrogance and wrong priorities.

IF ATHEISM IS TRUE...: THE FUTILE FAITH AND HOPELESS HYPOTHESES OF DAWKINS AND CO.

A former nuclear scientist turned missionary, Brian draws together some of his previously published writings on apologetics to produce a concerted offensive against what the apostle Paul would surely describe as the 'indefensible' arguments of the so-called 'New Atheists'. The short chapters in Brian's conversational style serve as an ideal entry-level primer for anyone wanting to get to grips with one of the most important of today's debates.

HEALTHY CHURCHES: GOD'S BIBLE BLUEPRINT FOR GROWTH

As Brian notes in the opening chapters of this book, many churches in the Western world seem to be declining in numbers and spiritual vitality. He explores some of the root causes and also how this trend could be reversed. The good news, as Brian reminds us, is that God gives us the growth blueprint in His Word through a number of key Bible words, such as sowing, reaping, planting, watering, cultivating, building and edifying. Find out the importance of each step in the process and get inspired to go for growth with, in and through, God!

TAKE YOUR MARK'S GOSPEL!

As Brian explains, Mark's Gospel answers the two most important questions that can engage the human mind - who is Jesus is and why did he die? That makes it essential reading for us all - and this accessible commentary unpacks all the key elements as well as providing study questions after each chapter for individual or group study.

ONCE SAVED, ALWAYS SAVED? THE REALITY OF ETERNAL SECURITY

The issue of whether a "born-again" Christian can lose their salvation is an absolutely critical one and has been a controversial topic amongst Christians for centuries. Brian provides a number of faith lessons which include insightful illustrations and Biblical references that all Christians can use to reassure themselves that there is no basis in the Bible for the so-called "Falling Away Doctrine". "For by grace are you saved, through faith."

GET REAL: LIVING EVERY DAY AS AN AUTHENTIC FOLLOWER OF CHRIST

Do you ever feel like you're just playing at being a Christian? Perhaps you even feel a bit of a fake or even a hypocrite - but you don't know what to change or how to change it. Here is some helpful, practical and scriptural guidance on Bible study, personal and collective prayer, worship, church life and family life, with the goal of us becoming authentic, credible disciples who live with real integrity!

ABOUT HAYES PRESS

Hayes Press (www.hayespress.org) is a registered charity in the United Kingdom, whose primary mission is to disseminate the Word of God, mainly through literature. It is one of the largest distributors of gospel tracts and leaflets in the United Kingdom, with over 100 titles and many thousands dispatched annually. In addition to paperbacks and eBooks, Hayes Press also publishes Plus Eagles' Wings, a fun and educational Bible magazine for children, and Golden Bells, a popular daily Bible reading calendar in wall or desk formats.

If you would like to contact Hayes Press, there are a number of ways you can do so:

By mail:c/o The Barn, Flaxlands, Royal Wootton Bassett, Wiltshire, UK SN4 8DY

By phone: 01793 850598

By eMail:info@hayespress.org

via Facebook: www.facebook.com/hayespress.org

www.ingramcontent.com/pod-product-compliance
Lightning Source LLC
Chambersburg PA
CBHW031408040426
42444CB00005B/462